Warning

This is the second book by the author
who wrote
Bill Oddie's Little Black Bird Book.

Bill Oddie's

GONE BIRDING

METHUEN

First published in Great Britain 1983 by
Methuen London Ltd
11 New Fetter Lane, London EC4P 4EE

Copyright © 1983 Bill Oddie

British Library Cataloguing in Publication Data

Oddie, Bill
  Gone birding.
  1. Bird watching—Great Britain—Anecdotes,
  facetiae, satire, etc.
  I. Title
  598'.07'23441   QL690.G7

  ISBN 0-413-51860-4

Printed and bound in Great Britain by
William Clowes (Beccles) Limited, Beccles and London

Contents

Glossary *page* vii

Introduction ix

1 Why am I a bird-watcher? 1

2 In the beginning 20

3 Growing up – a bit 32

4 Bartley Reservoir 44

5 Branching out 75

6 Observatories 100

7 Trapping and ringing 118

8 Cley 145

The last bit 180

Glossary

There are some birding terms that I haven't been able to stop myself using in this book. The most frequent are:

Twitcher – a bird-watcher obsessed with seeing rare birds and who chases all over the country in their pursuit. A twitcher will often use the following phrases (but that doesn't mean that I am a twitcher):

Dip out – to fail to see the bird you wanted to see.

To string – to misidentify a bird and not realise it (or at least not admit it).

To burn up – to search an area thoroughly for a particular bird you want to see.

To be gripped off – to miss seeing a rare bird which others have seen; *or* to grip off someone else – to prevent another birder from seeing a rarity by giving him false information, or no information or (even) by frightening the bird away.

A dude – a posh bird-watcher, who may not know all that much about birds. Nice people, and genuine bird lovers.

For a fuller explanation of these and many other esoteric matters I can only refer you to *Bill Oddie's Little Black Bird Book*.

However, *this* book isn't about twitchers (they've been done now!).

Introduction

THE SCOTTISH ORNITHOLOGISTS' CLUB

THE SCOTTISH CENTRE FOR ORNITHOLOGY
AND BIRD PROTECTION

21 Regent Terrace, Edinburgh EH7 5BT   Phone: 031-556 6042

22ⁿᵈ June 82

With Compliments

Dear Bill Oddie —

Thought you would

appreciate our first

refusal as 'Bill Oddie's Little
In addition I am returning 'Bill
Black Bird Book'. I was under the impression
that this book is about blackbirds.

Sincerely

C Harting

West Germany

This letter was forwarded to me by the Scottish Ornithologists Club's Bird Book Shop. It was my first refusal, and it was entirely justified. Although I could have argued that in the picture on the cover I did have a female blackbird sitting on my head, I certainly couldn't claim that my first book was about blackbirds, or indeed about black birds. Come to think of it, it was hardly about birds at all. Bird watchers – yes. Bird watching – certainly. But birds – hardly at all! Clearly I needed to write a second book. This is it.

1
Why am I a bird-watcher?

Before getting down to writing this second book I thought I'd better re-read the first one just to make sure I didn't repeat myself. As I began to skim through the glib but cheap pages of *BOLBBB* (short for *Bill Oddie's Little Black Bird Book* [now only £1.25 in paperback] and also, appropriately, a passable phonetic rendering of the mating call of the Black Browed Albatross), I was soon struck with a suitable sense of shame. Not only is it not about blackbirds, it is almost entirely about other people: i.e. I am forever slagging off some poor harmless dude or pitiful demented twitcher; denegrating the writers of other books and, most dangerous of all, bitching about other show business personalities. This *is* dangerous, as show business personalities are liable to bitch back – and they're often awfully good at it! In the very first sentence on page 1 of *BOLBBB* I have the unmitigated arrogance to claim 'Bill Oddie is the only proper "show biz" bird person'. Now this is of course perfectly true, but it is also a statement that has provoked many letters from all over the world. As it happens, none of these letters have come from other show biz

bird people – this is to be expected as none of them are
interested in birds enough even to read my book. So stuff
them! No, the letters have come from international ornithologists, and they have usually been asking the question: 'Who
the hell is Bill Oddie?!' I was privileged to receive correspondence from Don Roberson, undoubtedly one of America's
leading experts and author of the superbly erudite *Rare Birds
of the West Coast*. His letter began: 'Dear Bill Oddie, I have
never heard of you'. He went on to complain that his local
book club had had the 'unmitigated gall' to invoice him to
the tune of $20-odd for a book which he considered to be
'garbage'. He was of course talking about *BOLBBB*. Just to
make me feel really guilty, he then sent me a free copy of his
Birders California. This is a very entertaining and slightly silly
little book about American twitching – which I'd recommend, except that you can't get it in Britain! I realised then of
course that Don was only joking, and that he really
considered *BOLBBB* to be a masterpiece. I was able to
confirm this in November 1981 when I actually met Don
Roberson, believe it or not, at a sewage farm in southern
Sinai. He chased me halfway across an Israeli minefield asking
me for his money back. A whacky bunch, we birders, aren't
we? Anyway . . .

I have received the enquiry 'Who are you?' not only from
the United States but from New Zealand, Australia, South
Africa, Germany, Scandinavia and Golders Green. This kind
of ignorance does not offend me at all. After all, these people
have at least *read* the book, and such is the genuineness of my
concern for birds that any disappointment at my lack of
international fame is well outweighed by my satisfaction that
ornithology has a much more widespread appeal than silly
comedy shows. Still . . . for you unprivileged birders reading
this second book in underdeveloped countries without
television: that is what I do for a living. I do silly comedy
programmes.

For the past twelve years or so I have principally been on a show called *The Goodies* (I have been known, God help us, as 'a Goodie'). In Britain, at least, quite a lot of people watch *The Goodies*. Whether they *like* it or not is another matter. It does mean though that my name and, worse still, my face, is known, as it were, throughout the land. By the way, I know I promised to write about birds this time and there's three pages gone already. I'll come round to them eventually – honest I will. But I did sort of imply that I was also going to write about *me* instead of other people. So that's what I'm doing now – having a look at me, the bird-watcher. To do this maybe first I need to examine me the person, or rather, for the moment – me the so-called TV personality. I think it is arguable that TV personalities are not really people . . . or at least we're often not treated as people. I can understand it, mind you. As a Goodie I have over the years appeared before the public dressed as a rabbit, a mouse, a Swedish *au pair* and a tube of toothpaste. Almost never as a person. I suppose therefore I can't expect to be treated as one. If a bunch of kids see me walking down the street it must be rather as if Bugs Bunny has leapt out of the television set. I suppose I am a real-life cartoon character. Not surprisingly, they don't quite know what to do with me. What they usually do is embarrass me. I am easily embarrassed – which must sound like an odd statement coming from a man used to being dressed as a toothpaste tube. But it's true. An idiot on screen and a hermit off it, almost. I am also naive. I simply tend to forget that my face is known and accordingly I potter off innocently shopping or to the zoo with the kids and am constantly surprised when people stare at me or nudge one another. Actually probably they're embarrassed too. 'God, he has the nerve to go outside after that rotten show last night!' Anyway I'll admit I've never got used to it all. Basically I suffer from a kind of 'claustrophobia' brought on not by confinement of space but by being recognised. I once saw

Woody Allen being interviewed and he said, 'I used to get this funny feeling that people were following me – then I realised . . . they were!' I don't get as many as Woody Allen, but I know exactly what he means.

By and large people don't so much follow me as walk past and yell once they are at a safe distance. Often this takes the form of simply singing the first line of the Goodies' theme song – a sort of personal 'station identification'. It isn't remotely offensive but it always makes me feel terribly self-conscious. What is more intimidating is the ones who get fifty yards past, then turn and point, and announce to the rest of the world: 'Oi! Look! it's one of the ★★★ing Goodies!' They then disappear into thin air, leaving everyone in the street to turn and stare at me. The most skilful at this form of embarrassment are lorry drivers and London cabbies. They usually yell from the safety of their cabins whilst stopped at the lights and then drive away to reveal me cowering on the street corner. Blokes on building sites are terribly good at it too. I often can't even tell where the bellowing is coming from – somewhere up there amongst the girders. I totally sympathise with women who get exactly this type of attention. Such is male arrogance in general that a lot of men assume that women are flattered by being harangued with such gallant and gracious compliments as 'Wahey, darlin'' and 'Oi, wallop!' delivered boldly from the top of fifty-foot scaffolding or a passing lorry cabin. Most of the women I know find it uncomplimentary at the least and, at worst, irritating and offensive. Frankly, it often drives them nuts. It's really unfair on women – they can't help being women ('And men can't help being men?' – oh come on, that's *no* excuse!) But I guess I can help being a 'Goodie'. So maybe it's my fault. I suppose this is why I often feel so guilty about my resentment. If anyone says, 'Well, you've asked for it,' I can't honestly deny it. Certainly by and large most 'recognition' noises are basically amiable (and should be rather satisfying). I know all too well that the supposedly correct show biz reaction is 'the day people don't recognise me – that's when I'll be worried'. That's absolutely right and God knows I've tried beaming and waving and singing 'There's No Business Like Show Business' – but it doesn't work. Every time a bunch of schoolboys leaps out at me and goes 'Oo Oo Oo – The Funky Gibbon!' I just want to fall through the ground. By the way, for underprivileged birders who don't have radios or record-players either, and for younger readers, I had the misfortune to write and perform a truly humiliating but highly successful pop song called *The Funky Gibbon* which reached number 2 in the British hit parade in 1975. It is an achievement I have lived to regret, in the same way I rather regretted doing a coy little commercial for a MacDonald's hamburger competition in 1982 which for several months provoked members of the public to cry out at me, 'Oy Bill, how's your Big Mac?' or exort me to 'Have a go!'

So – I'm not very good at being recognised. Do I do anything about it? I have developed certain aversion techniques; one is talking to myself as I walk along in the hope that people will think I'm barmy and give me a wide berth. Another is pretending to be asleep. I'm particularly good at this on trains. I actually like travelling on trains but at the same time I dread it. Once spotted I am completely trapped. Many's the time I have cringed in the corner of a carriage whilst an entire trainload of schoolgirls and skinheads filed past and either giggled or barracked me. My defence is to curl up in a fetal positon and keep my eyes clamped shut, rather like a hedgehog. The girls cough loudly and the boys prod me. Often they discuss my identity.

The conversation I most enjoyed occurred when I was pretending to be flaked out in the compartment of an old-fashioned local train. It had no corridor and I thought I was safe there, having drawn all the blinds and barricaded the doors with my suitcase. Nevertheless, at one stop a lady got in and at another a gentleman. As far as I know they'd never met each other before but curiosity in me soon brought them together. Eyes closed, I heard this exchange:

'Is that . . . *him*?'

'No.'

'It *looks* like him.'

'No, he's fatter.' (Long pause.)

'*I* think it's him.'

'Hmm, it does look like him.'

'What's his name?'

'Bill Goodie.'

'Yes.'

'No. Oddie. Bill Oddie.'

'Oh, yes. Bill Oddie.' (Pause – to see if I reacted to the name?)

'No – it's not him.'

'No.' (Another pause.)

'There's a name on his case. Shall I have a look?'

'Yeh. What's it say?'

'Bill Oddie.'

'Bill Oddie! . . . It's the same name.'

'And it does look like him.' (Longer pause.)

'It can't be him though. *They* don't go on trains!'

OK, so now I've confessed I'm a raving paranoiac and I go through much of my life quivering with claustrophobia and wishing I wasn't me. What's all this got to do with bird-watching? Well, whenever I've been interviewed on radio, TV or by the newspapers about my birding interests, I'm invariably asked: 'Do you go bird-watching to get away from the pressures of show business?' Well, I suppose the answer would have to be: 'Yes' and 'No' (sometimes I think I'm confused about everything!). Certainly it's true that birding is a great relaxation and an antidote to the whacky whirl of entertainment, but what these interviewers tend to assume is that I took up birding in order to escape. I think this

may well be true in the case of many of the show business
bird persons – and a good idea too! – but in my case it just
isn't so. I have been birding since I was about ten years old
and whatever I was escaping from as a small boy it wasn't the
pressures of show business!

As it happens, I have always preferred birding either alone
or perhaps, better still, with only one companion. Even if I set
out in a group of three or four we tend to split into pairs and
then get together at the end of the day . . . that's a nice way to
do it. I've never much gone in for bird club coach outings and
I do have a bit of an aversion to mass twitching (though not
on any moral grounds). I think the truth is I have always been
an unsociable little blighter (grumpy almost!) and a bit of a
loner. My work and so-called fame over recent years has
probably hardened that tendency. But it's always been there.
Mind you, there's one recognition story that really pleases
me. A few years ago I went down to Cornwall – on the train
(they *do* go on trains!). One afternoon I was crawling
through the copse at the southern end of Porthgwarra – a
famous Cornish birding spot. I'll admit I was enjoying being
on my own and was a bit narked when I heard a voice
behind me:

'Er . . . excuse me . . . don't I know you?'

I must have been in a good mood (birding often puts me in
one). I didn't run away and I didn't pretend to be asleep. In
fact I noticed the bloke was wearing binoculars – all these
years of bird-watching have made me very observant – and
so I was disposed to be basically polite to a fellow enthusiast.
Actually I went a bit coy even:

'Er, well, yes, probably you . . . er . . . may have seen me
on television . . . you know, "The Goodies".'

The reply came: 'No – I don't watch television.'

'Oh well, then I . . .'

'No, I remember.' he exclaimed. 'Yes, I know who you
are!'

I was almost nervous – had I molested his sister? Or cut up his car?

'Yes, you're the bloke who showed me an American Wigeon at Cley in 1967!'

Now that's the kind of recognition I like!!

There's another question the interviewers usually ask and this is: 'Why birds?' meaning why watch birds, as opposed to flowers or trees or animals. I am sure every birder would have a different answer to that one, and ultimately it seems to me it's always a bit of a mystery as to why anyone has any particular hobby, as opposed to any other. In my case some of the obvious answers *don't* apply. It wasn't a childhood influence – I didn't have any 'birdy' relatives or neighbours – and neither did I live in the country. Nor have I ever had a particularly highly developed sense of bird aesthetics. I mean I don't find birds *ugly* (though many of them are – have you ever seen a young Wood Pigeon? – and I don't think a Coot is up to much) but neither am I too frequently awestruck by the sheer loveliness of a bird to the point of not bothering to age, sex and identify it first. Nor have I ever been through my 'Blue Tit period'.

To a considerable number of bird-lovers in Britain there needs be little more to their hobby than the appreciation of Blue Tits. 'Those cheeky little Tits have been at the milk bottle tops again!' Such topics have accounted for lengthy correspondence in *The Times*, sociological documentaries on TV and photographic spreads in a thousand wildlife magazines. Whole industries have prospered devoted entirely to the feeding, breeding and bathing of Blue Tits. So great is the demand for Blue Tit portraits that there are many bird artists who have found it unnecessary to learn how to paint any other species. Any school competition asking for twenty words on 'My Favourite Bird' will come up with a couple of Owls, a Kestrel and six thousand Blue Tits. Robert Dougall has based an alternative career on them; and 'tits like coconuts' must be the indisputed champion of the bird lovers' saucy joke contest. Frankly, a medal should be struck to the Blue Tit in recognition of its services to membership recruitment to the RSPB. I dare say there are members who believe that the black and white bird with the funny beak on the RSPB car sticker is a rather poor monochrome representation of a Blue Tit – and if it isn't, it should be! I'd have to agree Blue Tits have a lot going for them, but I have also to admit, cynic that I have always been, that I have never managed to anthropomorphise Blue Tits into 'cheeky little chappies' any more than I can really see Puffins as 'stout old gentlemen in dinner jackets'!

It wasn't the 'charm' of birds that got me into it. Exactly what kind of birder I am (an unromantic one?) and why I watch birds will perhaps emerge to you and indeed me in the course of working through this book. I really don't know 'why birds?' but one thing I do know is that the element I've always enjoyed about bird-watching is the unpredictability. You rarely know what you're going to see. I suppose it follows from this that I've always been particularly attracted by migration and vagrancy. Most of my formative birding years were spent in almost obsessional study of a regular patch. I was intrigued by the comings and goings of summer and winter visitors, and I was constantly on the lookout for something unusual – whether it was a rare individual, a notably large flock of a common species or a particularly heavy visible migratory movement. It seems to me that this unpredictability is something bird-watching has over most other wildlife studies. Plants and trees don't move much and even animals are usually known to be present in a certain area even though they may be incredibly difficult actually to see. But being able to observe them, given enough information, practice and luck, is relatively predictable. Many insects do, I suppose, have migratory wanderings as lavish and mystifying as birds, but somehow they don't 'grab me' in quite the same way . . . maybe they're not big enough!

Fish do it too – but I am a rotten swimmer – I tend to drown a lot. Obviously I don't mean in any way to denegrate the skills and thrills, of botany, lepidoptery, zoology, marine biology, or any other form of natural history study. One man's Caelocanth is another man's Yellow Bellied Sap Sucker! All I'm trying to convey is that, for me, one of the major excitements of going birding is to be able to say to myself: 'I wonder what I'm going to see today?' and never know the answer. Ornithologically I am an eternal optimist, so I always think it's going to be something unusual; and just now and again it is.

As I said earlier, I developed a pesterer deterrent of talking to myself, but even that isn't a recent quirk. If I'm honest, I've always done it! Whenever I go birding by myself I carry on a sort of running commentary – sometimes almost out loud but usually muttered under my breath. I suppose it sounds a bit like a cricket commentary. It usually starts with a fact and wanders into fantasy:

'Mmm . . . interesting . . . wind direction . . . light south-easterly . . . could just be local coming off a depression . . . on the other hand there could be a ruddy great anticyclone over the Low Countries in which case we just could be in for something good . . . what's that? Lesser Whitethroat? . . . only saw flick of its tail but . . . I bet it was . . . and at that moment it leapt up on the bush and . . . come on, come on where are you? come on show yourself. . . yep, there we are – Lesser Whitethroat – thought so . . . pretty impressive that. Nice bit of spotting. Lesser Whitethroat doesn't breed around here – must be a little "fall" . . . Ah ha! Whinchat on the gate post. Yes . . . it's looking good . . . and hello hello . . . thunder! – Ah ha, a ha! Yes, yes . . . light south-easterly, thunder clouds . . . perfect Black Tern weather . . . and as I climb over the fence and head back towards the reservoir – what do I see? Gliding in over the dam – twenty Black Terns and a Whiskered!! Nope. Two Black-headed Gulls . . .'

I suppose the commentary helps to whoop up an impression of excitement out of something that is pretty often deadly boring – just like cricket, come to think of it. I started commentating when I was a young lad and I still do it. The other thing I started doing fairly early on was keeping notebooks. Like most bird-watchers, I carry a scruffy little notebook for my on-the-spot field notes, descriptions and so on. Then when I get home I write it all out neatly in my Proper Big Notebook. My first proper notebook is dated 1956 and was started just after my fifteenth birthday. I had been birding for quite a few years before that and I'm sure had kept notes somewhere but alas they have been lost. So my official birding memoirs are contained in sixteen volumes from 1956 to the present day. Some of the early ones are appallingly scruffy, others are really rather neat! Some are tatty old exercise-books whilst others are bound and embossed with an elaborateness which would do credit to a medieval monk! Over the years they have passed through various periods of literary style and presentation. In early volumes birding expeditions are recounted in a florid, eighteenth-century anecdotal style influenced, I think, by Samuel Johnson's Augustine prose (I suspect I was doing him for 'A' level at the time). They are dreadfully pompous. A lengthy account of a 'possible' Richards' Pipit at Dawlish Warren August 1956 concludes:

'Reference to the Handbook has not been made yet and therefore any positive identification is being delayed.'

This is followed by a later postscript:

'After consultation with T.J. Richards (Devon) and reference to the Handbook it was decided that the bird was probably a Richards' Pipit.'

Then later still, and after an attack of conscience, no doubt:

'The record cannot be said to be authentic as such decisive characters as the hind toe and the voice were not noted owing to the short time of observation and the unsuitable location.'

All of which adds up to total string! Looking back, the bird was a Skylark (wouldn't you know!). The point is though that I *can* look back on that bird . . . I know it was a Skylark because if I close my eyes I can literally see it – crest and all – scuttling through the grass on the edge of Dawlish Warren golf links. The fact is these notebooks spark off an almost photographic recall of the events they record.

Nine years later the style had deteriorated to a brevity close to shorthand:

'29 March. Bartley Reservoir. 3 G.C. Grebes. 1 Mallard.'

But if I close my eyes I can see those birds too. The events covered by my most recent books are even easier to see – as the notes are usually illustrated with sketches, little paintings and photo montages. I vowed that in this book I would indeed write about birds and decided to do so by trying to retrace my birding life, as it were. At first it seemed a daunting task. As I tried to think back over the years the first thing I remembered was the fact that I have a lousy memory. But as soon as I began to reread my notebooks it became easy. As I turned the pages, the birds literally flew back past my very eyes. I only hope you enjoy seeing them now as much as I enjoyed them then!

Goodies A selection of embarrassing costumes in which I have shamelessly cavorted before the public.

MY NOTEBOOKS

Early Period 1. Volume 1, August 1956 to March 1957. Green exercise book, cardboard cover. This is the first page of my first notebook. It tells of a 'possible Richard's Pipit' in Devon. The reproduction here is very small and the text hardly registers because it was written in pencil. This is a blessing, as the record was entirely 'stringy' and I shall be less embarrassed if you can't read it. (For a full confession, see p. 12.)

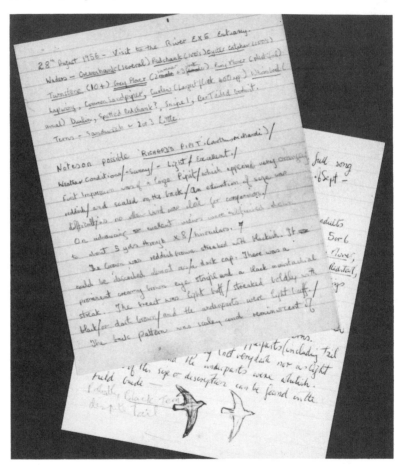

2. Also from Volume 1. Another dreadful early example of mistaken identification – or rather no identification at all. Early artwork is crucially inaccurate. What was it? Answer on p. 150; but please wait till you get that far – i.e. don't skip the next 140 pages, you *might* enjoy some of them! Note also waffly narrative style and immature handwriting . . .

WADERS at BLITHFIELD - Autumn 1962

WILDFOWL at BLITHFIELD - same period.

Middle Period 1. Volume 5, August 1960 to September 1962. Hardback, with red and blue squiggly design on cover, possibly intended for 'Accountancy'. Note how imagination decreases with maturity. Handwriting now vertical and neat. Wind strength, 24-hour clock times, abbreviations, graphs and no narrative whatsoever. Might as well have been written by a computer!

2. Volume 6, September 1962 to May 1965. Hardback, maroon. Middle period artwork, clinical but accurate. This is a juvenile Citrine Wagtail on Fair Isle. I actually *found* this bird but was never publicly credited, possibly because I had spent the whole day in bed – it was raining – and had gone out for a stroll only when the sun came out. By this time everyone else at the Observatory was soaking in a hot bath and trying to avoid catching pneumonia, having tramped around all day in the rain and seen nothing! It's possible they felt a bit narked with me. Life is so unfair sometimes, isn't it?

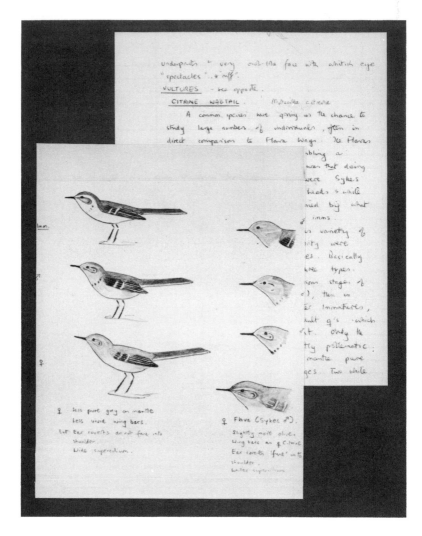

Later Period I. Volume 11, September 1977 to April 1979. Hardback, pale blue. The 'soulless' middle period lasted for nearly twenty years, until a trip to Bharatpur, India in February 1979. Particularly influenced by R.F. Porter (one of my companions), note-taking became obsessive. Here is a page of Citrine Wagtails, accompanied by five pages of notes involving accurate reference to feather topography, racial variation and 'confusion species'. Narrative style also reappears, with accounts of the Taj Mahal by moonlight and local curries.

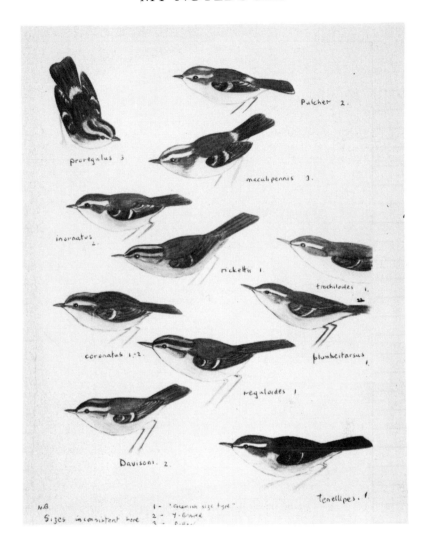

Later Period 2. Volume 12, April 1979 to June 1980. Also hardback, pale blue. Note how this more expansive style means I only got one year into one book. Artwork is showing pretensions of competence. Eleven 'Thai' Phylloscopus Warblers on one page – showing off, I'd say!

Present Day 1. Volume 14, 1981. Loose-leafed ring binder, maroon. It took me twenty-five years to realise ring-binders are the best and most flexible way of keeping bird notes, allowing for a combination of fancy artwork, borrowed photos and abstruse photostatted identification papers (the one featured here, by the way, being decidedly dodgy!).

MY NOTEBOOKS

Present Day 2. Volume 16, 1982, 1983 . . . A further and perhaps regrettable development – drawings and paintings now replaced with 'montages' of my own photos with lots of little notes by them. Efficient perhaps, but not quite so 'personal' . . .

The more recent examples, of course, all refer to trips abroad, which I'm not going to write about in this book . . . sorry about that . . . so, anyway, back to the mid–fifties. . . .

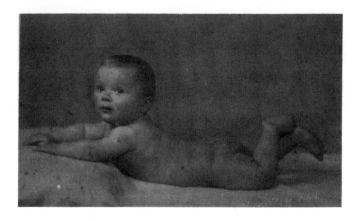

2
In the beginning

I was born in 1941 in Rochdale in Lancashire and that's where I lived until 1948. Rochdale was (and probably still is) a pretty typical Northern industrial town. It is famous only for being the home town of Gracie Fields and for being the first place in England to have a Co-op; it also boasts a rather nice town hall. Rochdale has never figured on the ornithological map and I have no recollection of ever seeing a bird there. I do remember living in a setting straight out of a Hovis advert. My house was at the top of a hill which had cobblestones that glistened in the rain and echoed to the sound of clogs worn by women in curlers and headscarves and men in flat hats. Down the end was a real cotton mill. It was called Sparth Bottoms Road. My home was one of a row of narrow houses in a terrace called, I think, St Alban's Terrace. There wasn't a lot of greenery around. We had a small stone backyard, with a tiny little enclosure of what I only remember as mud but which I suppose was meant to be a flower-bed.

There was some local habitat that should have attracted

some birds but if it did they didn't impress me at the time. Across Sparth Bottoms Road was an overgrown cemetery, no doubt belonging to St Alban's Church, which was probably a good place for Goldfinches and the like. All I remember about it was that several of the old stone graves had either collapsed or been vandalised and lay spookily open. I used to go and play in them. One day as I lay in my grave I saw a ghostly white hand waving out of another one. I ran away in terror, never to return. Presumably it was another little boy saying hello.

I was not unfamiliar with trees. Down the bottom of the terrace there was a fence and behind it a sloping wooden area with great big trees in it, but I was frightened to go in there too. A friend – maybe the same little boy from the grave? – had told me that there were wolves and tigers in the wood. I believed him. So I had no early experience of woodland birds. I did sometimes undertake expeditions to what almost passed as the 'countryside'. It felt like a ten-mile hike to a six-year-old but was probably half a mile away. I recall some stagnant ditches which were good breeding grounds for sticklebacks, tadpoles and rusty prams. Towering above the 'bog', as it was known, was a hillside of terrifying steepness where we used to go sledging. It was known as the Death Run. Looking back and trying to visualise that area, it may well have been quite a good place for birds. I remember none. Even right behind our row of houses there was a promising tract of urban habitat. This was a large, grassy common on which each year my gang built the biggest bonfire in the world and defended it in fearful stone-throwing battles against marauding rival gangs who came to steal the huge logs and tree-trunks from our fire. That common can't surely have been totally birdless? Or perhaps it was – I left Rochdale when I was seven and didn't go back until I paid a curiosity visit when I was twenty-one and fully grown (as fully grown as I've ever become.) I found Sparth

Bottoms Road all right but it wasn't cobbled and I saw not a single flat hat nor did I hear the clatter of a clog. The wolf and tiger wood seemed to have gone too – unless it was those two dead trees down the end. Just as I had grown, the 'common' had shrunk. It was no more than five yards wide. Presumably the bonfire had been a pile of twigs, I gave up on trying to find the Death Run – one little overgrown slag heap looks much like any other in those parts. On revisiting the area I could at least well understand why, as a small boy in Rochdale, I'd never been much attracted to birds. I still didn't see any. I did, however, see a rather sparse privet hedge running along the wall of the terrace in front of the houses and this jolted my memory of the only remotely or-nithological experience I had had during those early years. I remembered that I had found a Dunnock's nest in that privet hedge. It was made of mossy stuff and the eggs were turquoise blue. That's all. It wasn't a 'moment of truth'! I don't recall actually standing and marvelling at it or anything 'significant' like that. In fact, as it happens, turquoise is one of my least favourite colours, so if those eggs made any impression on me it wasn't a very good one. I have to confess I took one of the eggs and started an egg collection. As far as I recall, it remained a collection of one egg.

My other near-ornithological experience involved trying to add a second one. It wouldn't have counted, as it was a Canary's egg. I remember a friend (that boy again?) giving me a Canary's egg. I remember putting it in a matchbox in cottonwool. Then I remember putting the matchbox in the back pocket of my grey short trousers. Then I remember we had to climb over a stone wall – I don't know why – maybe we'd stolen the egg from a famous Rochdale Canary breeder. Then I remember getting home and reaching into my back pocket. Then I remembered I'd sat on top of the wall as I'd climbed over. So – the sum total of my birding experience in Rochdale between 1941 and 1948 was the establishing of a collection of one Dunnock's egg. At least I knew it was a *Dunnock*'s egg!

When I was seven my father changed his job. We left Rochdale and moved to Birmingham. Our new habitat was distinctly more rural, although I daresay it should properly be described as suburban. Even the name of our new road implied leafiness – Oak Tree Crescent indeed. The house was a pleasant semi and we had two gardens – a little one at the front and quite a big one at the back. This had a lawn and a vegetable patch, some apple trees and some rather nice straggly brambles along the fence. As subsequent years were to prove, it was quite attractive to birds. Especially Blue Tits! I certainly did put food and drink out for the Blue Tits but it wasn't, I'll admit, simply to enjoy their antics dangling on the nuts. Eventually my garden was to become a regular little trapping station, and Blue Tits definitely topped my ringing list; but that was some years ahead. In Birmingham, unlike Rochdale, I began to see birds right outside my house and this must have encouraged any budding interest I might have had. Oak Tree Crescent was in Quinton (it still is) on the very edge of the city sprawl and definitely within striking distance of fields, woods and lakes – real countryside! I grew a little, made friends and struck out to discover green places. In no time at all I was seeing birds and beginning to identify them. My source of reference at the time was *The Observer's Book of Birds*. There are now over forty *Observer's* books available, ranging from Fish to Flags to Furniture, but it is some tribute to our hobby that the very first one was *Birds*. This was published in 1937 and I doubt if the edition I was using in 1950 had been much revised since then! It was a little brown book (brown, that is, under the glossy paper cover which soon got torn or lost). It contained a rather indiscriminately incomplete selection of commoner British species, illustrated by antique little paintings more notable for aesthetic merit than usefulness. When compared with most of today's field guides, it is positively confusing. I did own a second *Observer's* book and a far more sinister volume it was, I'm afraid – *The Observer's Book of Birds' Eggs*. As a present-day council member of the R SP B it now behoves me to make a full confession of schoolboy crimes. If my resignation is demanded I'll understand it.

One of the principal motivations in my life once I'd moved to Birmingham was to add to my Rochdale collection of one Dunnock's egg. Like many schoolboys around me, I soon became an egg-collector on a fair scale. Were I to be active now I should be a prime target for the Species Protection Department of the R SP B – a group of ornithological sleuths who track down egg thieves with the thoroughness of Sherlock Holmes and nail them with the ruthlessness of the SA S. Egg-collecting is now quite rightly illegal. The R SP B's main concern is to catch the many highly destructive professional egg-thieves who are seriously endangering many vulnerable rare species, but technically and legally the schoolboy collector is just as guilty, and indeed just as potentially harmful to the birds. The message, frankly, is simple enough: collecting eggs is wrong. Nevertheless *I* was, in the late forties and early fifties, a schoolboy egg-collector and there is no way I can deny it. I can't justify the activity but I suppose I could attempt to defend my misdemeanours to a point. I wasn't then doing anything illegal, and I wasn't actually aware of any lobby against egg-collecting; I was always very careful not to disturb the nesting birds, and I only ever took one egg; and I knew what egg belonged to what species. Frankly, this was more than could be said for some of my fellow criminals – they couldn't tell a Barnacle Goose from a Budgie. Not that any of them had a Barnacle Goose's egg.

Anyway, there was a sort of country-walk circuit that I used to do regularly in those days. This is all before I started keeping notebooks and consequently my visual recall is a bit hazy. It is sadly perhaps significant that when I try to retrace my route mentally, most of my reference points are places where I found a particular nest. In view of my habit of carrying on a running commentary it's perhaps appropriate that my schoolboy birding (or rather egging) expeditions usually started on the cricket field. It wasn't actually a real cricket field but compared with the single chalk wicket on the garden wall outside my house, it was as impressive as the Oval. It was actually a large meadow with grass so long that any decent lofted shot would lose the ball for a couple of hours – which scored an automatic six! By contrast the playing strip in the middle had no grass at all. We didn't have proper wickets – we used milk crates – but there *were* two of them. So we had proper ends, and often up to five or six a side. For me there were two distractions from the game. One was a little girl called Marian who used to hide behind a nearby hawthorn bush, throw her knickers out and then 'streak' across to retrieve them. If you could coincide your run-up with Marian's appearance, you could more or less guarantee the batsman would take his eye off the ball – bowl a straight one and you'd got him. The other distraction was 'Skylarks'. There was a pair breeding in the meadow and my gaze would often stray from the on-coming bowler – or even Marian – as I watched a bird plummet into cover. At this point I would literally throw the bat away and, with eyes fixed on the spot, would set off into the long grass muttering: 'Don't distract me – don't distract me – keep your eye on it – two foot left of the dandelion.' I was often bowled out this way if the bowler cared to be unsporting. Neither did I have the consolation of finding the nest. Not, that is, until the day a batsman lofted a six and as it dropped the ball startled a Skylark from the grass. On retrieving the ball I not only discovered the nest but also learned a little about bird behaviour: that Skylarks drop down and then *walk* some way to their nests, thus making it a lot harder for schoolboys to find them and steal their eggs.

Anyway, having scored a double century, taken ten

Wildlife study . . . Skylark at nest . . . with cricket ball and nude.

wickets, admired Marian's performance for the sixth time
and checked on the Skylarks – which, I am happy to say,
usually raised their young successfully – I would then set off
on the rest of my country jaunt. This took me first down a
narrow path past some more meadows with considerable
hedgerows. This was the scene of my first remembered and
confessed stringing experience ('stringing' being birders'
slang for claiming to see a rare bird when you've really only
mistaken a common one). Actually I made *two* errors in those
fields, ironically both involving the same species. Somehow I
managed to convince myself that a brightly coloured bird
with a stubby beak and a white wing bar perched on top of a
tall hawthorn bush about a hundred yards away was a
Hawfinch. It was, with no doubt at all, in fact a male
Chaffinch. Then later that spring I heard what I recognised as
a Chaffinch's song coming from the top of the same bush (I
should have felt guilty about the Hawfinch already!). I was
surprised, however, to see the presumed Chaffinch fly up
from the bush, gain height and then deliver its song while
plummeting down on fluttering wings, then landing back on
the highest branch, adding 'tsee tsee tsee tsee' as it did so. I

remember making a mental note which sounds like the heading of an obtruse letter to *British Birds*: 'Chaffinch delivering unusual song in flight'. That was how I dipped out on a Tree Pipit! Which, of course, balanced up the stringy Hawfinch, so fair enough.

The path by the meadow lead down to a sort of parkland area which was fenced off as part of the grounds of a rather posh-looking farmhouse – it almost qualified as a country mansion. In front of the building was a very neat, round lawn and in the middle the most irresistible temptation any schoolboy can encounter – a huge conker tree. Each autumn it released a deluge of the biggest conkers you ever did see. I never met up with the owner of the house, but I was convinced he was large and ferocious and very cruel to schoolboys. There could be no other explanation for the fact that the lawn always seemed to be covered in conkers. Presumably everyone was too terrified to go and get them. Not me though – I used to scamper out, fill my cap and race back again, trembling in the knowledge that if I was ever caught I would surely be horsewhipped. As if this wasn't risk enough, one summer I discovered another temptation. The old house was covered in ivy and in it were nesting a pair of Spotted Flycatchers. A Spotted Flycatcher's egg was a priceless addition to any schoolboy's collection. I risked my life again and I'm sorry to say I got away with it. Carrying on past this dangerous farmhouse area, I continued down a dark little path through a tunnel of rhododendrons and emerged at the top of an open hillside looking down on the considerable expanse of the Leasowes Woods. I was intrigued enough by this area to get to know its variety of habitats and the corresponding birds extremely well. It was indeed pretty good. The slopes of the hill had a few large trees, some of them dead, and these were excellent for the farm Flycatchers and the odd Woodpecker. Down at the bottom the grass was longer and here I found the nests of Willow Warblers. Then the path lead to thicker woods, with a couple of small ponds, with more rhododendrons on the edge and some reedy patches. Moorhens bred there, and in winter there would be a pair of Grey Wagtails. There was a much bigger pool where people fished, but not wild-fowl. I don't think I ever saw a Duck or a Grebe on there. Sometimes I'd make a detour up a steep bank covered in thick, low hawthorn, brambles and gorse, and this was excellent for breeding birds – Greenfinches, Linnets, Yellowhammers and Whitethroats. Struggle to the top of the bank, and I'd emerge by the canal. I remember one day I saw a blue bird which flashed past me and the next time I saw an orange one. The third time I realised I'd seen the same bird each time – a Kingfisher! There's no doubt I was becoming more and more interested in the birds themselves, and I started keeping a list of how many species I'd seen, but still my main obsession was with finding the nests and frankly I was becoming pretty good at it.

The best area of all in the Leasowes was at the edge of the golf course. Here there was long uncut grass dotted with brambles and hawthorn bushes and overlooked by larger trees. Moreover, with the cropped fairways close by, it was always possible to find a good vantage point from which I could get a clear view of 'the rough' where the birds were feeding and breeding. I found many nests there and, I suppose, collected a number of eggs. There is some justice in the fact that it was also that place that lead to me getting my come-uppance for my wicked ways. One hot summer day – quite late in the year – I was half asleep, lying in the grass by the edge of the golf course. As far as I was aware of the birds at all, I was watching a pair of Willow Warblers feverishly bringing food to their youngsters in a nest which was obviously somewhere on the ground under a fairly sparse hawthorn bush. I was conscious enough of the birds' vulnerability not to wish to disturb the chicks, but eventually curiosity got the better of me and, after studying exactly where the birds kept going in, I crawled over for a quick peep. Before I got there I almost stuck my elbow in another nest . . . rather bigger than a Willow Warbler's and containing about a dozen golden-brown eggs as big as hens' eggs! I'd discovered a Pheasant's nest. I think I was vaguely aware even then that there was something a little odd about a nest having a full clutch of unhatched eggs so late in the season. Anyway, the egg-collecting urge came upon me and I even broke my usual rule and, I imagine convincing myself that pheasants can't count above half a dozen, I took three eggs, leaving what still looked like an awful lot. I must have been going visiting that day as I ended up with my eggs at a friend's house. I remember the scene extremely vividly.

'Just William' was on the television. (A serial I never missed. I suppose I felt a particularly close affinity with it as it was about a naughty, scruffy little boy with my name.) The telly was visible from the kitchen which is where I took my three eggs in order to blow them. I borrowed a pin and made the holes and began blowing out the yokes into the sink. I must have been in love with Violet Elizabeth or something, as I didn't notice till halfway through the second egg that there was a most appalling stench creeping through the house . . . beginning very close to me. My friend *had* noticed and so had his mother. Even 'Just William' was beginning to look a bit askance. If you've ever smelt bad eggs you'll know it's not a nice experience. Blowing them is far worse. Those eggs were well 'off' – they were evil – and I'd been putting them in my mouth! I've never had a great sense of smell and my sense of taste must have been pretty suspect – actually my sense of sense must have deserted me that day. Instead of instantly disinfecting the kitchen and chucking the third egg in the dustbin, I actually went on to blow it. It was quite a challenge. The foul and rancid contents had begun to thicken and I had to half suck as well as blow in order to empty the shell. But eventually I did it. I placed the third egg with the other two, carefully washed out the sink – and then threw up in it. The taste has stayed with me forever – writing about it now is bringing it back to the point where I'll have to stop very soon or risk ruining my manuscript. But good came of evil. I never took another egg again! I even destroyed the 'evidence' and threw away my collection.

Of course blowing a bad one is not the reason for not collecting eggs. Quite simply it's a destructive thing to do – it destroys young birds and endangers species. I certainly look back on my few years of schoolboy egg-collecting with considerable remorse. However, there was a more positive side to it, perhaps – I did learn many techniques that I was eventually able to turn to better use. I learned which eggs belonged to which bird; also colours, clutch sizes and so on. It's an area about which many birders are totally ignorant. I learnt a lot about which species nest where – the relationship of particular birds to particular habitats. Of course, I learnt how to find nests and this was a skill that I found invaluable in later years as a ringer, ringing young birds at the nest. But above all else, as I sat for hours watching the cautious and canny movements of birds to and from their nests, I did develop one quality essential to any bird-watcher – patience. It was a quality which I was to test to near the point of masochism during the next phase of my birding life.

1. Me – at an early age doing a very convincing impersonation of Les Dawson, doing a convincing impersonation of me at an early age. Note early interest in wild life.

2. Probably approximately aged five, perhaps. Note unwitting signs of an ornithological future – Fair Isle sweater and typical birding habitat – looks like the quay at Penzance, waiting to board the *Scillonian*, in October. (Actually it's Blackpool in July.) The grown-up is my Dad.

3. Aged about ten. The garden at Oak Tree Crescent before it became a major ringing centre.

4. An amazingly obvious Willow Warbler's nest in the Leasowes Woods – photo taken after the young had flown – honest!

3
Growing up – a bit

My memory for significant dates is not terribly good unless, of course, the particular event has been documented in my bird notebooks. Sometime around 1954 – when I was thirteen – I think I became a proper bird watcher. My promotion was celebrated or at least commemorated by my father buying me my first decent pair of binoculars. I'm not sure whether I had any binoculars at all before that and if I had they must have been ex-opera glasses or plastic toys from a Cornflakes packet. Whatever they were, they were so unmemorable that I have forgotten them. I knew I was going to get a good pair for Christmas but I pretended I didn't, and Dad went along with the pretence to the point of hiding the box and not putting it with the rest of my presents. That Christmas Day I feverishly worked my way down a pillow-case full of boys' annuals, games and jigsaws, hurling them aside ungratefully in my anxiety to uncover my 'big present'. I'm sure Dad enjoyed the look of disappointment, pique and disbelief on my little face as I frantically rummaged around the bottom of the empty sack: 'No binoculars! But . . . but

. . . but. . . .' Maybe my tears were just about to turn to aggression, because he suddenly gave in and guided me with a game of 'Warm . . . colder . . . colder . . . freezing . . . warm . . . hotter . . . very hot . . . burning!' to a brown-paper parcel hidden behind the settee. Inside it was a pair of brand new 'real' binoculars. I was so grateful I put them on, jumped on my bike and went out for the rest of the day, leaving him to enjoy his Christmas dinner in peace.

I don't know where Dad had done his market research but he had certainly chosen well. The binoculars were Barr and Stroud 8×30s – an excellent model even by today's high standards, and by no means cheap. Knowing the pushy little lad that I was in those days, I rather suspect I may have done a little research of my own and then told him exactly what to buy me. Which was why I wasn't entirely surprised to receive them. I suppose I had a bit of a nerve – but actually it was a wise enough piece of persuasion since those binoculars lasted me at least ten years – they are no doubt still going strong wherever they are – someone eventually had the good taste to steal them.

The second significant event of my thirteenth year was that I changed schools. Again it was my father who instigated the move and again it benefited my birding aspirations. My 'little school' in Birmingham had been Lapal Primary, a very nice school in a semi-rural setting where children were clean, polite, non-violent and generally well behaved. I was certainly very happy there. My main achievements to my mind were sporting. I played one game for the school football team as a goalkeeper. I was then moved to right-half before word got round opposing schools that I was only about three and a half foot tall. Amazingly I'd only let in two goals during my goalkeeping career – one under my body and the other, rather more predictably, over my head. A shot by which most normal-sized boys would have been winded in the belly!

I went on to represent the school many times at football and also I was a right little megalomaniac on the cricket field – opening both the batting and the bowling. As far as I was concerned, at the age of nine, I was destined to become a pint-sized Ian Botham. My father and the head teacher at Lapal, however, had another idea. They decided I was clever. This was embarassing enough, but to make matters worse I went on to prove it! At the age of nine and a half they put me in for the 11 plus (that's often made me wonder about the teaching of maths at Lapal Primary). Anyway – I passed. To be honest, I suspect most nine-year-olds would have passed the 11 plus if they'd ever got to take it, but they didn't. I did – *why* I shall never know. The result was that, when I was just over ten years old, I moved on to Halesowen Grammar School where I was to spend three fairly miserable years. Academically I continued to be objectionably successful and I was consistently top of the class. The problem was that I still wanted to be Ian Botham and Barry John and Steve Ovett, or whoever the equivalent sporting heroes were in those days – Dennis Compton, Cliff Morgan and Roger Bannister perhaps – or W.C. Grace, Prince Obelensky and Sydney Wooderson – how long ago was this? Well, I was at Halesowen Grammar from 1951 to 1954, I suppose.

When I arrived there I was just over ten and the rest of the boys were, on average, eleven and a half years old. At that age, one and a half years makes a hell of a difference on the playing field. To make matters worse, I was small for my age. Consequently most of my memories of Halesowen Grammar School involved being humiliated on the sports field. I remember trying to run a hurdles race and having to go under them. I remember being crushed by gorillas on the rugby field, and I recall being literally knocked out by a fast bowler who struck me with what I considered to be a vicious bumper but was probably a perfectly good length ball that would have just clipped the top of the stumps if I hadn't stopped it with my head! I remember escaping this continual battering by occasionally sneaking off looking for birds' nests and indeed trying to improve my knowledge of the birds themselves. Alas, I didn't get a lot of encouragement, as I failed to find any other boys with the same interests.

Then in 1954 my Dad decided to test my supposedly precocious academic prowess yet again by putting me in for an exam to the high school. I honestly had no idea what I was attempting to qualify for but since I wasn't very happy at Halesowen I went along with it and took the exam, and again I passed. So it was that in September 1954 I moved to King Edward's School, Birmingham. There were lots of King Edward's Schools around the Midlands but, to be entirely snobbish about it, they were all 'just' grammar schools – but *the* King Edward's School was supposedly a cut above that. Strictly speaking, it wasn't *the* high school either – that title went to the adjacent girls' school – King Edward's High School for Girls, Edgbaston. Pronounced Edgbarston or Edge'b'ston. King Edward's School, Birmingham for Boys – KES, B'ham – if I have to own up, was a public school. You didn't get in by passing the 11 plus. It had its very own entrance exam which was supposedly far more difficult. I tried to claim it wasn't a *real* public school because it wasn't a boarding school, but it did boast a very high standard of academic achievement. I soon discovered this as I plummeted from being top of the class at Halesowen to third from the bottom at KES! Nevertheless I was delighted with the move.

I was thirteen when I moved to KES and most of the boys had been there since they were ten. It might well have been hard to integrate at this relatively late stage but two special events occurred during the first few weeks which made everything pretty easy. The first incident occurred on my very first day. It was playtime – or rather 'break' – and I had brazenly joined in a game of football on the school parade ground. The ball ran loose on the wing and I and another boy chased after it. I got there first. The game stopped. Every player stared at me. I took advantage of the unexpected lack of opposition to slam the ball between the two piles of coats that passed for goal posts. As I floated back to the centre circle in slow motion I received no applause, but the boy who had chased after the ball with me approached me respectfully and asked almost reverentially: 'How fast can you do a hundred yards?' Well, the truth was I'd never got as far as a hundred yards at Halesowen. I'd usually scampered off in tears after floundering behind during the first few strides. The pain of being continually beaten had put me off athletics. I truthfully told the boy I had no idea how fast I could run a hundred yards. He simply went: 'Mmm,' and there was a lot of nodding and muttering amongst the other players. The game resumed with me being given far more of the ball than I could cope with. I didn't know why. As the bell went for the end of break I was taken aside and told the truth – in running for that ball I had just beaten the school junior hundred yards record holder! It was like a story out of *Boys' Own Paper*. Naturally we became the best of friends! In fact he must have been having a bit of an off-day, as I don't think I ever beat him again. Nevertheless, in no time at all I began to enjoy the exhilaration of being able to compete on equal terms with boys of my own age and some of them even my own size. Actually I never was anything but a bit on the squitty side – but I seemed to make up for my lack of inches with aggression and maybe even some expertise.

Anyway, the fact was most of my happiest days at KES were spent on the athletics track, the rugby field, the cricket pitch or the tennis court. My happiest days off were spent birding, and again it was the school that taught me how.

The second significant event of that first week at the high school was my discovery of the societies board. This was literally a large, green, felt-covered notice-board on which a variety of school societies advertised their activities and canvassed for new members. At KES school societies were largely organised by the boys themselves – not the teachers – and they covered a great variety of activities from chess to rowing, via the Shakespeare Society and the Jazz Club. There was a tradition at the school for designing rather lavish and elaborate posters for the societies board and one immediately caught my eye. It was covered with birds and was advertising the Natural History Society. I went to a meeting and – another revelation – I met lots of boys whose main interest was bird-watching. I have no doubt at all that I owe a great debt of gratitude to KES Natural History Society and I was very lucky indeed to be at the school at a time when it was flourishing. I recently received a letter from a present pupil bemoaning the fact that he is now the only bird-watcher at the school. In my day there were lots, from first year beginners like myself, still reliant on their *Observer's* books, to sixth form experts who discussed mysterious topics like 'wing formulas' and 'reverse migration'. The school itself was located close to an excellent bird area, Edgbaston Park, which includes a golf course, splendid mixed woodlands and a marshy-edged lake that even during my school years produced such Midland rarities as Black-necked Grebe, Common Scoter, Long-tailed Duck, Velvet Scoter and Ferruginous Duck. The Society organised a day-to-day census and survey of the Park which I myself eventually supervised when in later years I rose to the dizzy heights of secretary. However, in 1954, all that glory was still to come. During my first year's membership I acquired three things – companions, a copy of the then brand-new and revolutionary Peterson's *A Field Guide to the Birds of Britain and Europe*, and instructions on how to join the West Midland Bird Club.

My second great debt of ornithological gratitude must go to the West Midland. It was then and, I believe, still is the biggest bird club in Britain, and one of the best organised.

There were regular field outings to Midland reservoirs, coach journeys to the coast and even birding holidays abroad, and each month well-attended meetings were held at the Birmingham Art Gallery. Or so I'm told. The fact is I never once went on a trip or attended a single meeting! Yet for eight years from 1955 until 1963 the West Midland Bird Club motivated most of my birding activities. The irresistible attraction was the Annual Report. During the year, members sent reports of unusual sightings to the secretary and these would appear in the monthly newsheets or bulletins. It was nice to see one of your records in print, but not entirely satisfying because your name wasn't on it. However, in the Annual Report each record was credited to the observer, as it was followed by his or her initials. I still have a collection of WMBC annual reports. The oldest one is for 1956, and there is no little significance in the fact that the very first record on the very first page reads:

Black-throated Diver. One seen at Bartley Reservoir on December 23rd (W.E.O.).

WEO stands for W.E. Oddie which is, by the way, my full and correct name: not Bill Oddie, especially not if it's going to be reduced to initials!

The West Midland Bird Reports are built to last – nice strong light cardboard covers with glossy photos, good paper and secure binding. The birds and the initials that appear by them are indelibly part of Midland ornithological history. Remember, this is the biggest bird club in Britain, so thousands of members read and re-read these reports. They are, therefore, well aware of the efforts and expertise of prolific contributors. Little wonder that to a budding egotist like me, my prime motivation during my school years became how many times could I get my initials in the Annual Report? I am lucky to have slightly quirky initials anyway – WEO – it sort of stands out on a page of JSs, MPAs, JTs etc –

don't you agree? And it has a certain ornithological appropriateness, being a passable phonetic rendering of the call of a Wigeon – 'WEO' – or is it a Little Owl? Anyway, my initials appeared twenty-six times in the 1956 report, which wasn't a fantastic total; but in subsequent years I acquired considerable expertise on how to get more and more records accepted. The system was that, despite having sent in records for the monthly bulletins, you had to officially resubmit them all again for the report at the end of the year. This gave you time to add all sorts of obstruse observations that could well qualify to go into print and notch up another set of initials. You wrote out your records on little pink record slips. Most observers sent in a fair-sized envelope – I sent in a big parcelful. The majority of records were of unusual species – Midlands rarities – but there were all sorts of other ways you could boost your total. The most productive was to contribute heavily to the 'Arrivals and Departures' section. This was an appendix at the back of the report which recorded the three earliest arrival dates of spring migrants and the three latest departure dates, and the latest dates of winter visitors in spring and the earliest of their arrivals in autumn. Probably not that many people kept a personal log of such matters – but I certainly did! And consequently I often managed to dominate this section. My finest achievement was to score three initials of one species alone: Garganey (1963).

Garganey. Av. = April 7 (21)	Av. = September 9 (20)
March 15 Upton Warren (W.E.O.)	Sept. 29 Blithfield (G.M.I.)
22 Minworth (H.T.L.)	1 Belvide (M.M.C.)
24 Cannock (A.R.L., W.E.O.)	1 Upton Warren (W.E.O.)

Another good idea was to keep on visiting a long-staying rarity that had been found by somebody else – in the hope of getting your initials on its last sighting:

Great Northern Diver. From 1st December (A.R.M.B.) to February 12th (W.E.O.).

Ruff. Max 17 at Blithfield (W.E.O.).

Or you could count Gulls. Very few birders bother to
count Gull roosts so I used to go round all the Midland's
reservoirs at least once each winter and estimate the numbers
of the three or four species of Gulls roosting there. This gave
me a very good statistical likelihood of scoring at least a
couple of initials.

Herring-Gull. 2,800 estimated at Belvide roost on December 24th (W.E.O.).
Black-headed Gull. 1,000 at Bartley on November 22nd; and 2,700 at Shustoke
on December 23rd (W.E.O.).

Records of visible migration were always a good bet
('Common Gull: small numbers moved over Bartley on autumn passage (WEO)')
and reporting unusual plumages was usually worth a try. Most
albinos would make it into print, and I was indeed fortunate to
have secret knowledge of a melanestic Kestrel which made the
report for three years running.

Kestrel. Dark-coloured specimen again seen on several dates at Bartley Green
(W.E.O.).

One advantage of studying the same area for several years is
that you can make authoritative comparisons –

Field fare. Commoner than last year round Frankley (W.E.O.).

– and if you're really pushed you can actually boost your
score by not seeing a bird at all.

Little Owl. No records from Frankley (W.E.O.).

During my first few years sending in records I became
increasingly expert at all these techniques as is proved by my
consistently improving scores in the WMBC annual reports.
From my twenty-six initials in the 1956 report I soon got to
forty-eight the following year. In 1959 I broke the magic
fifty and in fact hit sixty-two initials. I peaked in 1960 with
sixty-nine and then showed remarkable consistency for the

following two years, at sixty-eight in '61 and sixty-nine again in '62. My drop to forty-eight in 1963 was explained by the fact that it was in the autumn of that year that I left Birmingham and moved to London. In fact I had left school in 1960 and from 1960 till 1963 I was at Cambridge University. My Midland birding was therefore reduced to holidays only during these three years. During that time I kept up my initials tally by getting around more and during the school holidays I made daily circuits of as many Midland reservoirs as possible, which, in the West Midlands, is quite a few.

During my school years, however, my approach had been quite the opposite. One sure way of guaranteeing a large number of published records is to become the regular local expert on one particular place, so that the vast majority of records from that place are likely to have your initials on them. If, however, you choose a really *good* place, you may find yourself competing with lots of other regular bird-watchers. The trick is to choose somewhere really dreadful. You may not see much of interest but you can be more or less certain that anything you *do* see will be seen by you alone, and will therefore bear *your* initials. At a really dull location even the commonest birds can be noteworthy and earn a place in the report.

Turtle Dove. 1 at Bartley, where unusual (W.E.O.).

I managed to find an area so rarely visited by birds that it was almost never visited by bird-watchers, a place so boring that for years I had it almost to myself. It was the perfect local patch.

1. Lapal Primary School 1st XI Football Team – Spot the Oddie Contest. (A clue: I was no longer the goalkeeper.)

2. King Edward's School Birmingham 2nd XI Cricket Team – I was drummed out of the first team for 'slogging'. The 2nd Team consisted entirely of sloggers and was unbeaten all year – the 1st XI drew every match! PS I am *not* the captain . . .

3.

4.

3. KES 1st XV Rugby Team – and I *am* the captain; so there.

4. Edgbaston Park Pool – within two minutes walk of school; a splendid habitat made all the more attractive by the fact that I had to walk past the girls' netball courts to get to it.

4
Bartley Reservoir

The village of Bartley Green is about five miles south-west of the centre of Birmingham. Bartley Reservoir, constructed in 1931, is of the impounding type formed by a dam built across a natural valley. The maximum height of the embankment is 65', the top water surface of the reservoir about 117 acres with a length of about two-thirds of a mile and a maximum width of about 630 yards. Its capacity is 541 million gallons. The embankment is formed of earthwork obtained from inside the reservoir and has a central core wall of reinforced concrete extending below ground in a trench 6' wide to a maximum depth of 60'. The water slope of the embankment in the region of the top water level and the whole of the marginal slopes are protected against wave action by concrete paving.

This is a quote from *The Birds of Frankley and Bartley* by W.E. Oddie of History 6th, KES, for which he won the Bowater Natural History Prize in 1958. This erudite work consists of forty pages of graphs, tables, notes, check lists, theories and conclusions: the main conclusion being that Bartley was a big concrete reservoir with very few birds on it. A not untypical entry in my notebook records:

'January 12th 1957: very windy and cold. No ducks or anything on the reservoir.'

Exactly a month later the situation hadn't really improved: 'February 12th 1957: still nothing.'

It is a remarkable tribute to my patience that five years after that I was still keeping meticulous records.

'30th March 1962: No fowl (only more so).'

Of course the truth is birds did occasionally visit Bartley: 'April 4th 1962: one Lesser Black-backed Gull. One Lapwing.'

Whenever they did, I recorded the event, and I was never reluctant to publish my observations.

As well as the world-renowned Bowater Prize essay, I wrote an authoritative paper for the West Midland Bird Club that was either so long or so amazingly dull that it was spread over two consecutive annual reports: 'Birds in the Bartley Reservoir Area (1931 to 1962) Part One', WMBC Report 1962, was followed in 1963 by the much anticipated 'Birds in the Bartley Reservoir Area (1931 to 1962) Part Two', both by W.E. Oddie.

My full accounts are contained in six volumes of notebooks from 1956 to 1963. They faithfully record every visit, and there were a lot. From September 1956 to September 1960 I visited Bartley on 309 days. There were concentrated peaks especially during school holidays and particularly in 1960 when I went to the reservoir every single day in both May and August. From 1960 to 1963 I spent my terms at Cambridge University but was back home for the vacs during which I racked up a further 155 visits, including another peak of every day in August 1961. Many of my visits were literally from dawn to dusk. The total number of hours

I spent at Bartley is almost horrifying. I daren't work it out,
but I have calculated that during my school years I spent an
average of 1½ days of the week at the reservoir. I was at school
5½ days a week. Posh schools go on Saturday mornings. On
Saturday afternoons I'd be out playing rugby, cricket,
athletics or tennis for the school teams. Every Sunday I
would spend birding, and during the holidays I went to
Bartley, birding, nearly every day. Considering this schedule
it strikes me that I can't have spent much time at home! What
was it that drove me to prefer the concrete wasteland of
Bartley Reservoir to the family joys of our semi in Oak Tree
Crescent?

Home life during my teens was not so much unhappy as
. . . dull. I was an only child and was consequently relieved of
the distraction and responsibility of having brothers or sisters.
Mind you, I also felt deprived of their company. My father
had left his school in Rochdale at the age of fourteen, become
an apprentice in a light bulb factory and worked his way up
to assistant chief accountant at, appropriately, the Midlands
Electricity Board – thus retaining his connection with light
bulbs. My mother had not lived with us since I was a baby,
and therefore most of my Dad's life had been devoted to
bringing me up. Like many self-made men of his generation,
he wanted to make sure I was given the education he never
had. He succeeded. It was much more due to his guidance
than my intellectual ability that I went to King Edward's and
eventually to Cambridge. I am entirely grateful to him as it
was at these two establishments that I learnt to develop fully
my lifetime's obsessions and enthusiasms. KES taught me
about birds, and Cambridge taught me how to write silly
songs and shows. My father was eternally supportive during
my teenage years and, frankly, I lacked for nothing to the
point of being spoilt. He bought me not only binoculars but
also a telescope and a bike. He also gave me lifts in his car, and
I remember him cooking most of my meals for me. He took

pride in my exam results when they were good and was greatly distressed when they weren't; and he avidly collected the write-ups in the local papers recounting my exploits on the rugby field. I am sure he lived not so much *with* me as *for* me, and perhaps even *through* me. I am sure I did not really appreciate it at the time but I certainly do now. I am extremely indebted to him; yet I can't help feeling that by involving himself so completely in my life he sadly neglected his own. He didn't go in much for social activities, apart from playing the occasional bowls or darts match, and I rarely remember him inviting workmates to the house. There was, mind you, another reason for this. Dad and I were not alone.

My Granny lived with us and had done as long as I could remember. My Granny looked like a small ape. She was very tiny and wore her hair scraped back from her forehead and fastened in a little bun at the back of her head. Her round, crinkled face was thus framed by a helmet of grey, flat fur. This style exposed her ears which were fairly prominent. Her beady little eyes were accentuated by round, wire-framed glasses and her false teeth seemed rather too big for her mouth which forced her lips out into a protruding per-manent grin, typical of the aggressive facial expression of a cross chimpanzee. If she managed to close her mouth she appeared rather more serene. She was then perhaps more reminiscent of a Rhesus monkey. She didn't actually swing around from the light bulbs, but she was indecently active for her years. She was nearly eighty at the time I first became fully aware of her and something over ninety when she died when I was, I think, about sixteen or seventeen. Although she was not really physically or mentally capable of running the home, she refused to recognise the fact. As far as she was concerned she was the woman of the house and intended to fulfil her duties. She would insist on attempting to cook meals and she tried to do all the washing and cleaning, often falling over in the process. Unlike many grannies, she never

went off to her own room. She was always downstairs
burning the supper or tripping over the Hoover. Or
interrupting our conversation. She simply couldn't and
wouldn't be left out. My father never told me the facts of life
and we rarely had any man-to-man talks, and I'm sure this
was because we could never be alone together. Granny
would follow us everywhere. Some nights Dad and I would
sit silently for hours, determined that we'd have a chat after
she'd gone to bed. She never did. Sometimes she would fall
asleep in her chair but we still couldn't talk. The sight of her
false teeth slowly slipping from her lips and ending up in her
lap was too entertaining and distracting, and anyway she
snored so loudly as to drown any attempt at conversation. If
we tried to slip away into the kitchen she'd wake up
immediately and follow us. She also broke wind frequently
and very loudly. It was something we'd got used to, and
indeed rather enjoyed – but my father understandably had
decided not to subject his friends to such an unsociable
experience.

As well as our rather cluttered sitting-room we did have
what was referred to as the 'front room'. It should have been
the 'lounge' – the place where Dad could invite his mates
back for a drink and a game of cards. During my Granny's
lifetime, however, it was never anything but a junkheap –
full of old teachests, musty books and festering wellies.
Whilst Gran was alive the front room remained a mess and a
symbol of just how completely the old lady dominated the
atmosphere. To be honest, I could appreciate my father's
surrender – a farting Granny is a great deterrent to gracious
living! It was not insignificant that a month after she died
Dad cleared up the front room, bought a nice powder-blue
three-piece suite and a mahogany drinks cabinet, and threw a
small party for his chums from the office.

Before that liberating gesture, in the same way that Dad's
social life had been inhibited, so too was mine. Certainly I

don't remember having many friends back to the house –
presumably because there wasn't really anywhere for them to
go. I did have lots of friends, but I used to go to their homes
instead.

Although I had a Granny, I didn't have any other relations.
There was an aunt and uncle who had moved from Rochdale
about the same time as we did, I think, but they had gone
even further away down to Hampshire. As far as I can
remember we never went to visit them and of course no-one
came to visit us. Neither did we have family holidays, I
presume because Granny would have had to come with us,
which she couldn't, so we didn't. There were absolutely no
family gatherings at Oak Tree Crescent and certainly no
grand reunions at Christmas time. Indeed Christmas Day at
home always ended in tears. Usually, I fear, my father's. He'd
plan to cook a Christmas dinner, but Granny wouldn't let
him – she'd insist on helping. I don't remember much about
the results except I do have a vivid mental picture of soggy
sprouts (that must have worked wonders for Granny's
flatulence!). So on Christmas Days there would be a
traditional Yule Tide row, then Dad would give up any
attempt at seasonal festivities and fall asleep in front of the
telly; I would hop on my bike and go off to Bartley. My
notebook recalls lots of birds seen on 25 December. Whatever
the shortcomings of my home life, I am most grateful to it – it
drove me to bird watching! Or rather it drove me to Bartley
Reservoir; or rather I cycled there.

As it happens, I do remember cycling there for the very
first time – or at least I remember the birds I saw there. It was
a most untypical visit, as there *were* a lot of birds on the water.
I haven't got an accurate count of the species, as this historic
event occurred actually some time before I started keeping
notebooks. It is, however, some measure of how memorable
that day was that I can, nevertheless, still close my eyes and
see again what I saw that day sometime in the winter of 1954

or 1955. I recall parking my bike by the reservoir railings opposite what looked like a good-sized pack of wild-fowl about thirty yards out on fairly calm water. Propping my monstrous brass Broadhurst Clarkson telescope on the railings, I panned along left to right and began my commentary:

'Mmm, quite a nice little flock out there . . . mainly Tufted so far . . . ah, Pochard . . . and more Tufted . . . Mallard . . . and Wigeon . . . and more Wigeon . . . quite a lot of Wigeon . . . a couple of Teal and several Shoveler . . . oh, about a dozen Shoveler, that's nice and . . . Pintail . . . wow! . . . that's good . . . two males and a female . . . and more Tufted and . . . hello . . . small Grebe . . . Slav or Black-necked? . . . er, smudge goes below the eye, and bill slightly up curved . . . Black-necked – I think . . . yes definitely, excellent . . . and more Pochard and . . . what the hell's that? . . . big black shiny duck with yellow on the beak . . . never seen one of those before . . . yes I have . . . in the book . . . Common Scoter . . . drake Common Scoter . . . nice one . . . yes, not bad at all.'

Not bad indeed! That would be a pretty impressive selection for any inland water. For Bartley it was a bloody miracle . . . but I didn't know it then. I'd never been to Bartley before so as far as I was concerned that might well have been a pretty average population for the reservoir. The truth is that in 464 visits over the following ten years, I never saw anything like it again!

I used to cycle to Bartley on my bike, which was a rather flashy steel-blue Dawes with dropped handlebars and a saddle that I never was able to lower enough to enable me to get my feet on the pedals properly. I kept my Barr & Stroud 8 × 30s dangling round my neck, which meant that if I used the drop handlebars properly, the binoculars got tangled up in the bell or gear lever and slowly throttled me. To avoid this I had to sit upright and hold the handlebars along the top instead, so there was no point in them being dropped at all. Neither did I have a basket on the front or a saddle-bag at the back. I carried my telescope and packed lunch in a small haversack. I refused to wear this properly as it looked a bit prissy, so I butchly slung it over one shoulder. As I cycled it continually slipped off and dangled dangerously near the spokes. I should, of course, have bought a sensible bike, but that would have been soppy.

The ride to Bartley was really quite pleasant; about three or four miles, I should think, and mostly downhill. My route took me through a mixture of the new housing estates and farm fields. No doubt now it is *all* new housing estates but it could then be fairly described as semi-rural – one degree better than suburban. I emerged from the newest of the housing estates onto the brow of a hill overlooking the reservoir itself. It was possible to scan the water from this spot, and within about one minute be fairly confident that it was absolutely devoid of birds. However, I was never so pessimistic. I chained my bike to the railings and set off on foot on a circuit that would take me around several areas of different habitat adjacent to the reservoir. By the middle of the morning I might still have found very few birds worth noting but it would have taken me at least three or four hours to have done it. I was in fact very devoted to my circuit. It was rather like doing the rounds at a bird observatory. I always managed to whoop up a little thrill of anticipation as I approached any particular area, commentating as I went, and as time went by

I got to know the specialities of each location, modest though most of them were. My usual route took me down the road overlooking the reservoir from the west side. If I was lucky, I'd be distracted by a few dots on the water, and if I was very lucky they'd turn out to include an uncommon duck, Grebe or even a Diver. Just now and then a Tern or two would be skimming the waves, and even a few Gulls would be enough to constitute a worthwhile day.

In my survey reference system Bartley Reservoir itself was Area A. Rather perversely, I'd next have a look at Area C. This was twenty-five acres of mixed deciduous trees known as Bromwich Wood. I never saw anything really rare in there but it attracted migrant Warblers, especially in spring along with the occasional Redstarts or 'Flycatchers. Next came Area B. This was Frankley Reservoir. I never did quite understand Frankley Reservoir. I think it had something to do with the water-purifying process of the nearby filterbeds. It was in the shape of a perfect semi-circle with vertical stone walls running round it and therefore no shore line. Anything landing on the edge would have slid down the wall and drowned. Any bird on the water would have felt as if it was in a big, stone bath and got raving claustrophobia. Birds, logically enough, seemed to hate Frankley. I once saw a lone, confused Whooper Swan swimming around honking, but it was a young bird and presumably hadn't learnt any sense. There was a narrow dam or causeway bisecting the reservoir on which there was always a dejected little huddle of Mallard and a single Lesser Black-backed Gull. I felt fairly confident that it was the same demented Gull that stayed rooted to the spot for ten years. The saving grace of Frankley was the closely cropped lawns below its stone walls which were invariably the place Wheatears chose to make their first appearance in the spring, usually earning me a set of initials in the 'Arrivals' section of the Annual Report.

With little sense of symmetry, I would then continue from Area B to Area D. This was Westminster Farm, in many ways my favourite spot. The main attraction was a small pool with a nice little reed bed and a clump of willow trees and sallows. It really did feel like a bird observatory there, as in spring and autumn a daily watch would notch up a fascinatingly fluctuating number of Warblers and, indeed, many years before my time, the West Midland Bird Club had for a while operated a small Heligoland trap in the nearby farmyard.

From Westminster Farm, Area D, I trekked up the hill to Area B, Frankley Beeches. This is a well-known Worcestershire landmark, being a large clump of very tall beech trees perched on top of the highest point around and visible for miles. It was a wearying and dull climb up to the Beeches, and rarely worth it. There was a nice view of several counties but rarely any birds up there, except in a Brambling year. Bramblings do like beech trees and consequently Frankley Beeches was a logical place to look for them. From 1956 to 1963 there were no Brambling years!

From Area B I'd usually retrace my steps and do the whole thing again in reverse, until I'd qualified for the reward of a bacon sandwich and a cup of exquisite milky coffee at a transport café in Bartley Green Village. Then, if I was feeling really adventurous, or couldn't face going home to Granny, I'd either do the whole circuit yet again from A to E or, just once in a while, I'd strike out for the mysterious regions of Areas F and G. G was known as Bromwich Fields, and consisted of large areas of wheat and barley in summer and stubble in winter. It was most worthy of a visit during hard weather for flocks of Buntings or Fieldfares and Redwings. F was Twiland Wood, which was much the same as Bromwich Wood, only a lot further to walk. By covering the whole of the survey area from A to G and back again, I

1. Looking down from Frankley Beeches – Bartley Reservoir on the left, Frankley on the right. The Lesser Black Back is on the end of the central dam.

2. Bromwich Wood. Note the empty road – this photo was taken at dawn just before the invasion of learner drivers.

3. Bromwich fields, with cows put out to lure Yellow Wagtails.

4. Westminster Farm. Pool complete with Winchat fence.

could quite happily spend a whole day from dawn to dusk
seeing very little indeed. I often did stay out all day as the
entries in my meticulous notebooks testify:

'17th January 1959: 0745hrs to 1600hrs.'

'3rd January 1955: 0845hrs to 1300hrs: foggy all day.'

That then was my Bartley circuit. Certainly over the years
I saw some birds but I surely worked for them, and, as if their
scarcity wasn't challenge enough, finding them involved
putting myself through another ordeal.

There is one sound that always brings back memories of
bird-watching when I was a kid. It isn't the call of the Wild
Goose or the cry of the Seagull, it is the sound of a farmer
going: 'Oi!!' At Bartley Reservoir there was also the dreaded
water bailiff. The whole of Bartley Reservoir was fortified
by a ring of viciously efficient iron railings with spikes on
top. There were lots of *PRIVATE* notices threatening fines
and torture to trespassers, and the forbidden grassy banks
were patrolled several times during the day by the water
bailiff. I suspect that he had a personal hatred of bird-watchers
and possibly of birds, and that he was heavily armed.
Reading back through ancient copies of the West Midland
Bird Club reports, there were historic tales of vast Gull roosts
at Bartley, and in days of old it had been one of the best
reservoirs in the Midlands for wintering flocks of Golden-
eye. But these were long gone and I was convinced it was the
water bailiff who had driven them away.

I personally witnessed him at work several times. The
moment a Goldeneye or anything else so much as splashed
down on the water, he would gallop round the banks of the
reservoir with a big Alsatian and frighten it away. Several
evenings Gulls attempted to form a roost and were bombar-
ded with exploding shells which rained down on them like a
royal fireworks display. At various points along the reservoir
there were several small rocket-launchers armed with anti-

Gull missiles. The official explanation was that the Gulls fed on rubbish dumps during the day and in bathing before roosting were washing off pollution into the water. Since Bartley provided drinking water for most of Birmingham, this was considered to be a serious health hazard. I reckon all this was simply an elaborate front to cover up the fact that the water bailiff had a thing against birds, bird-watchers and particularly me. The wonder of it is that over the years I still managed to notch up quite a decent tally of unusual wild-fowl but, not surprisingly, none of them stayed very long. They used to drop in for a few minutes and either get bombed by the bailiff or else they'd soon realise that the waters were as unproductive as the Dead Sea and off they'd go again. During their brief stays and the bailiff's tea-breaks the birds were easy enough to see as there were absolutely no reeds, lilies or mudbanks to hide behind. Where wild-fowl were involved the bailiff was a deterrent, not a danger. It was the Waders that got me into trouble. Occasionally in spring or autumn I'd hear the piping of a Common Sandpiper or even the squeak of a Dunlin, and their occurrence was so infrequent that I was certainly not happy unless I could actually see them. Alas, this was almost impossible as they'd skulk craftily along the bottom of the sloping concrete shoreline, totally invisible from my position behind the railings. At first I tried belting round to the other side of the reservoir and looking back across the water – the birds were then just about visible, but 200 yards away, so I couldn't identify them properly. The frustration was too much to bear and eventually I'd attempt to squeeze between the railings and cower behind a clump of dandelions, listening for that inevitable call: 'Oi!'

Such is the vocal power of water bailiffs and farmers that their 'Ois!' can be projected at small boys from anything up to five miles away and still induce heart-failure. If I didn't instantly pass out, I'd hurl myself at the railings like a frustrated chimp in a zoo cage until I found a gap big enough to squeeze back through. I'd often get jammed or I'd attempt to climb over and get stuck on top of the spikes. Perhaps I should have stayed perched on the fence, because if I dropped back into the field I'd hear another 'Oi!' from the farmer who owned it. Strangely though, I was never actually caught by the water bailiff. Even more strangely, I never tried to ask his permission to have access to the banks of the reservoir. I think I was convinced he wouldn't give it, as it would have meant me having a key to unlock the heavy-duty double padlock on the gates. I've a feeling I was right, but I should have at least asked.

Dodging the water bailiff was pretty nerve-wracking and usually left me trembling for hours. I used to calm down by pottering off to my favourite spot, Westminster Farm. There I could sit by the side of the road, where I was quite safe, as long as I didn't get run over, and watch migrating Warblers in the willow-clump. Unfortunately one day I was tempted by a cow. The cow had wandered down to the edge of the stream by the reed-bed and as it gaily paddled and mooed it flushed ten Snipe, three Teal and a Water-rail! None of these birds would have been visible from the roadside. I couldn't always rely on a passing cow, so next Sunday under the barbed wire I went. It didn't *say PRIVATE*, and I convinced myself that the fence was there to keep the cows in rather than bird-watchers out. I crawled along the side of the marsh, crouched down quietly in a cow pat and waited for the Water-rail to appear. Suddenly I heard a familiar sound: 'Oi!'

'Water-rail giving unusual call,' I commentated.

Then there was a crashing of foliage from behind me as if King Kong was lurching through the jungle. The cow? Please let it be the cow. No such luck. The 'cow' picked up my big brass telescope and bonked me on the head with it.

Ever been bonked by a Broadhurst Clarkson? A bit more memorable than these modern plastic jobs, I can tell you.

'What are you doing?' bellowed the farmer (which at least proved that farmers could say something other than 'Oi!').

What was I doing? Since I had a pair of binoculars, a telescope and a notebook I felt like saying, 'Guess . . .' but I didn't. Instead I cringed a lot and said very meekly: 'I'm bird-watching, er . . . is it all right if I walk along your field . . . Sir?'

He bonked me again. There is, of course, a moral to all this. Bird-watchers should always ask. This story doesn't even have a happy ending. The farmer replied: 'No, it's not all right,' walked off with my telescope and, within a month, he began filling in the marsh as a rubbish tip. Nowadays I *think* the lesson has sunk in and I try to be absolutely meticulous about asking permission. The fact is most local water authorities will happily issue bird-watching permits for reservoirs and sewage farms. An increasing number of farmers are sympathetic to birders and will allow access to their land if approached civilly beforehand. Mind you, I can hardly blame the ones who are not so co-operative, as they must be heartily fed up with trespassers damaging fences and crops and, alas, there is no denying that sometimes birders have been involved. There certainly *is* a worrying minority of irresponsible bird-watchers, but then again there is also an equivalent minority of paranoid farmers. The trouble is, the rules of trespass in the countryside are so ambiguous and the sign-posting so inconsistent that it often really is difficult to know the rights and wrongs. By and large I find birders these days very well behaved, and it worries me that they are sometimes treated rather neurotically as if they were an invading army of dangerous and destructive freaks.

Some years ago I was coming back from a summer holiday and having landed about mid-day at London airport I decided to pop into Staines Reservoir. There I met another birder who asked if I'd been to see 'It'. I hadn't, because I didn't know what 'It' was. Well, 'It' turned out to be a Black-winged Pratincole (silly name!) which had been present for a few days in the area of some gravel pits near Reading. Reading isn't far from Staines so I drove off to try my luck. I'd been given excellent, precise instructions of how to find the bird. They led me down a path along by a canal and up to a railway embankment. I then went over a stile and walked along the embankment which overlooked some stubble fields and an area of gravel pits. I sat down on the top of the bank. I didn't instantly see the Pratincole but I did spot a gaggle of frantic bird-watchers gesticulating violently to me to get out of the area as quickly as I could. Was I about to be shot at or blown up? I hurried over and asked them. The answer was much worse. Apparently I was in grave danger of being sprayed with manure! The farmer whose land the Pratincole had chosen to frequent had such an aversion to birders that he had been thundering up and down all day in a high-powered muck-spreader, spattering them with cow dung! I'll admit I've never heard the farmer's side to this one, but the fact is I certainly wasn't aware that any of the Pratincole's fans were trespassing (me included) and certainly there was no damage being done.

There's a reasonably satisfactory ending to the tale. I joined the remaining intrepid birders for a patient vigil at a spot about half a mile away from the gravel pits on an indisputably public road. As we waited, a plume of smoke began to rise in the distance, swelling to a raging wall of flames – the farmer had literally set fire to the railway embankment in order to deter the bird-watchers. It also deterred the Pratincole, which was soon smoked out of hiding. It headed purposefully in our direction and gracefully came into land in the field right in front of us.

Nevertheless, the sound of 'Oi!', let alone muck-spreaders, still haunts me every time I go out into the countryside. I assume I'm trespassing even when I'm not. I'm almost incapable of climbing over a stile without looking furtive. Opening a five-bar gate always makes me feel guilty, and I still can't get used to the fact that I don't need a permit to get into Minsmere now that I'm on the council of the RSPB. Every time I go there I have to fight a strange criminal urge to crawl under the barbed wire. Maybe I'm really a pathological trespasser. I do still get told off quite a lot. Last time I went to Farlington Marsh Reserve I managed to walk across a forbidden field and was properly admonished by a polite but efficient warden; and I got a right earful at Blackpill! Blackpill is in south Wales near Swansea and looks pretty much like an ordinary bit of seaside. However, because of the sewage outlet, or some such unsavoury attraction, vast flocks of Gulls gather there and these often include rarities. Most notably in recent years it has produced a series of records of that uncommon Yankee visitor, the Ring-billed Gull.

About five years ago I visited Blackpill one September afternoon to see if I could tick off a Ringed Bill. It was low tide and there was a vast expanse of mud and an even vaster expanse of Gulls. There were also several joggers, shell-collectors and dogs scampering across the beach, and each time they neared a flock of birds the whole lot would get up, flap around and come down a hundred yards away. Normally I don't really fancy wandering about aimlessly at low tide. I prefer to wait until the birds are concentrated by higher water and then scan through them methodically. However, this time there seemed to be so much disturbance I felt I may as well set off there and then. The beach wasn't, of course, private but I was aware that I was breaking some kind of ornithological rule and I felt positively guilty as I slipped on my wellies and plodded across the sand.

I felt even more guilty ten minutes later as I heard that familiar cry: 'Oi!' It came not from a farmer nor indeed from a water bailiff. This particular 'Oi!' had a Welsh accent and came from the Secretary of the Gower Ornithological Society (funny that all these species have the same call, it makes them very hard to identify). To be honest, I may not have got exactly the right title for this particular gentleman and if he ever reads this account I apologise, but whatever his official title, he was an eminent and authoritative Welsh birder and he *was* shouting 'Oi' at me, and he was pretty cross. I shuffled over to where he stood imposingly astride a concrete parapet at the edge of the sea-front. I bowed my head and struck a suitable pose of admitted but repentant guilt, like an Italian footballer trying to avoid the yellow card. But he wasn't going to let me off with a caution. He lectured me in strong Welsh tones on the ethics of birding at Blackpill:

'Was that you out there scaring all the birds away?'

No point in denying it, he'd seen me. 'Yes.'

'That is *not* how we do it here, look you. No, we sit at the edge and wait for the tide to come in. All the birds are forced nearer and nearer and they all come right in front of us and we get a much better view. There is absolutely no need to walk across the beach. If you do, everything flies away.'

I agreed that this was the considerate, logical and probably most efficient way to watch the area. I sat with him as he calmed down and we spent a pleasant hour in increasing drizzle as the tide came in. By the time it had, we were soaked, but we had had fairly good views of a couple of Curlew Sandpipers and a couple of thousand Common Gulls. He bade me a cheery farewell: 'See, that's how to do it. Bye bye.' I apologised again and thanked him. I simply couldn't bring myself to admit that when I'd walked out across the beach almost the first bird I'd seen had been a sub-adult Ring-billed Gull! Mind you, I'd taken his lecture to heart. I went back to Blackpill a week later and was too nervous to do anything but sit and wait for the tide, as he had instructed. I didn't see a thing.

Ringed-Bill Gull.

Anyway, talking of not seeing anything . . . back to Bartley Reservoir in the mid-fifties. Understandably, I had the place more or less to myself in those days – other bird-watchers would drop in from time to time, scream with boredom and drive off to one of the many much better places no more than half an hour away. Nevertheless, I was not entirely alone in my strange masochistic obsession. In browsing through current West Midland Bird Club reports I had noted another set of initials related to Bartley – GHE. Rather strangely, most of GHE's records were waders. This was a double surprise as I had not seen any other regular watchers there and I very rarely saw any waders either. However, one autumn day both mysteries were solved. I'd found a new place to trespass. I'd been exploring a wooded gully at the north-west end of the reservoir when I came across a previously undiscovered section of iron railings that seemed to exist for no other purpose than to be climbed through. It was quite possible to get round them at either end, but much more exhilarating to squeeze through a gap that some super-human being had created by forcing two of the spikes apart. So through I went and followed the path which emerged at a small sheltered grassy hollow by the edge of the reservoir, which was quite invisible from back up at the road. Lying in the hollow was GHE. George Evans. We introduced ourselves and began to chat, and the conversation lasted on and off for the next two or three years.

George, more than anyone, should be given the credit for proving to me that even a godforsaken wasteland like Bartley can produce very interesting birds. My memories of George Evans are probably inaccurate but I'd imagine he was in his mid-twenties when I was about fifteen and I think he'd been in the RAF before moving or returning to Birmingham and, for reasons best known to himself, deciding to make Bartley his local patch. How on earth he ever noticed it I never knew, but he had discovered that Bartley was on some kind of flight path or inland migration route for waders. Since the banks of the reservoir were solid concrete, the birds had the good sense not to bother to drop down and attempt to feed on them. Very wise too. Any wader attempting to plunge its beak into the Bartley shoreline would have ended up badly bent (any Midland records of Terek Sandpiper would no doubt refer to Redshanks who made a silly mistake at Bartley – obstruse birding quip). Nevertheless George had recorded a very nice variety of species – flying over. Usually they appeared high over the north dam and disappeared off to the south-west. Possibly they were passing across Britain on a line from the Wash down to the Bristol Channel. Hopefully they would call a few times, which was often the only indication they were there at all. If they were flying they might not be visible or they were at least very hard to spot. Luckily quite a few of them *were* spotted, by George Evans, and *he* showed them to *me.* The numbers were not large, even by the standards of other Midlands reservoirs, but compared with the couple of Common Sandpipers I'd had up till then, they were phenomenal. Dunlin or Ringed Plover were predictably the most frequent, though rarely more than half a dozen singles in a day, whilst Whimbrel and Greenshank occurred in small parties. There was a flock of nine Ruff in August 1957, three Black-tailed Godwits in 1959 and a Bar-tailed in 1960. The odd Grey Plover and Knot were unusual for the Midlands, and I suppose the best bird was a Purple Sandpiper in September 1957, which even risked landing on the concrete for a few minutes. To bird-watchers used to the prolific wader flocks at estuaries or coastal reserves, or indeed mud-fringed inland reservoirs or sewage farms, these events must seem somewhat unimpressive. To me, in those days, how-ever, they were fantastic rewards for hours and hours spent lying in that hollow gazing at the sky or half-dozing with eyes closed but ears always alert. In 1960 I went to Bartley every single day in August and on the 31st I was rewarded with a Bar-tailed Godwit, a first for the reservoir. To me then that Godwit was as satisfying as a first for Britain would be now.

George Evans and I often shared these long vigils together, and talking birds with him guaranteed that the hours were anything but tedious. The longer we watched, the more visible migration we discovered passing over Bartley. Oc-tober was particularly fascinating when small flocks of Skylarks and Meadow Pipits would appear over the dam and then fly south-west low over the waves, exactly like long distance migrants do over the sea.

Observations in other parts of the West Midlands, Wales and the West Country discovered a widespread movement of birds, generally to the south-west, culminating in them leaving Britain from Land's End bound for the continent or southern Ireland. Again the scale was modest, but clearly

Bartley Reservoir was, in its own little way, involved in this general movement. Of course in amongst the common migrants just now and again would come the local rarities – a Twite, a couple of Snow Buntings or a Short-eared Owl. George showed me what was going on over Bartley, and I continued to document it for years. Certainly my observations earned me many a set of initials in the report, but my fascination for migration was geniune enough and it was amazing the satisfaction I could get from recording a couple of Meadow Pipits flying south-west.

Sometime in the mid-fifties George Evans left the area. I haven't seen him since, but I do know he spent some time as warden of Bardsey Island Bird Observatory, so his expertise and dedication was certainly not wasted. Until 1960 I had Bartley pretty much to myself and I suppose I became the local expert, a mantle I had sort of inherited from George. It wasn't perhaps a fantastic claim to fame but I think I was pretty proud of it at the time. I suspect my reputation must have spread a little, as on 14 February 1960 I was approached by a young schoolboy bird-watcher. He was suitably deferential and polite: 'Are you Mr Oddie? I was told to get in touch with you.' By whom, I never did find out. My notebook records the occasion:

'February 14th 1960: met Andrew Sp.'

Sp. is bird-watching shorthand usually applied to an unidentified species but in this case it meant I hadn't remembered his surname. It was, in fact, Lowe – Andrew R. Lowe – A R L – initials which were soon to overtake mine in the annals of Bartley Reservoir's history as recorded in the WMBC reports.

Andrew was also destined to become my long-term birding companion and we shared many bird adventures for the next fifteen years or so . . . but these are tales still to be told. Meanwhile, in 1960, I left King Edward's School and went off to Pembroke College, Cambridge University. It can

only be a comment on my relative incompetence that no
sooner had I left Bartley than the birds began to improve. I
kept in touch with Andrew who was forever rousing my
jealousy with reports of a flock of sixteen Greenshank and a
Spotted Redshank and, most galling of all, a period in late
January 1963 when Bartley produced a Velvet Scoter, two
Snow Buntings, an Arctic Skua and an Iceland Gull – all
ARL! Not that I didn't have some good birds myself
(curiously enough, many of them came during my university
holidays, during which I always raced faithfully back to
Bartley). Maybe the birds *did* improve during the early sixties
– or maybe *I* did! During the fifties I suppose my best bird
was a Marsh Warbler singing at Westminster Farm on 1 June
1958. I also have many happy visual memories of Divers –
Great Northerns and Black-throateds – and a flock of
fourteen Bewicks Swans, a pair of Pink-footed Geese flying
over, an immature Velvet Scoter and a drake Smew. 1961
was a good year, when a Quail took up residence in a corn
field behind Bromwich Wood and, being a Bartley regular
and therefore trained to super-human patience, I was one of

Marsh
Warbler ...

the few people ever actually to see it. Hundreds of people *heard* it, but I *saw* it. In late August 1961 I had one of my nicest Bartley experiences – lying on my back. I had in fact fallen asleep in the grass on the eastern side of the reservoir. I awoke and as my eyes focused vertically upwards, way above me, I spotted a close formation of dots in a clear blue sky. For a moment I wasn't sure if they were midges or birds, but they plunged ever downwards, finally fanning out over the reservoir and revealing themselves to be a party of twenty-eight Black Terns. By the end of the day there had been two more small flocks, adding up to a total of forty-five for the day, another Bartley record, and not bad for anywhere inland.

In summer 1963 I left Cambridge University. In October I also left the Midlands, moving to London to take up my accidentally new-found career in show business as part of the cast of that year's university Footlights Revue. (It was called *Cambridge Circus* and was the first Cambridge show to move straight into a West End theatre. Its cast included eventual co-Goodie Tim Brooke-Taylor and embryo Pythons Graham Chapman and John Cleese. If you're curious about this seedy other life it's all documented in a rather fascinating book called *From Fringe to Flying Circus* published by Methuen.) From 1956 to 1963 Bartley Reservoir had been an obsession. During those years I put in thousands of hours and saw a few birds. I never had a sniff of a proper rarity. Nothing that even qualified for 'Recent Reports and News' in *British Birds*. When I look back over the pages and pages of my neat little notebooks recording almost nothing I can't help wondering *why I did it*. It wasn't as if there weren't several other good reservoirs within cycling distance or at least a bus ride. If I'd worked out a sort of ornithological league table of Midlands waters, Bartley would have been due for relegation. So what *did* I get out of it? It can't just have been the ego trip of being the West Midland record holder for the number of initials in the Annual Report (I'm not even sure I was anyway). Neither can it have entirely been the vanity of being considered an expert on an area most bird watchers didn't think worth visiting. I'd like to think that the reason I did it, and enjoyed it, was in fact that I was aware that the whole experience was doing me good. It was my 'training', a tough kind of apprenticeship, a bit like going to an Outward Bound School (which, by the way, I did; and whose unofficial motto was 'When it hurts it's doing you good' – very like Bartley). What Bartley really taught me was to do with the immense satisfaction that a birder can get at having a local patch. Most of the birds I found at Bartley were *my* birds.

I soon learnt to scale down the whole business of rarities – a Grey Plover at Bartley is as rare as an Upland on the Scillies. A Lesser Whitethroat is as good as an Icterine Warbler. Anyway, in those days I didn't do so much travelling that I was aware of such real rarities. In a sense I suppose I didn't know what I was missing, so I didn't miss it. This satisfaction in finding my own birds is something I'm still a bit obsessed with. Nobody seems to believe me when I say I'm not a twitcher (if you've managed to avoid knowing what a twitcher is, see the glossary at the front of this book; or, for a fuller explanation, read *Bill Oddie's Little Black Bird Book*). I suppose because I wrote about twitching at some length in the *LBBB* other birders understandably assume that I have done my fair share. Well I have, but that was mainly during the sixties and early seventies. Nowadays I must admit I find I don't get much satisfaction from travelling to see a rarity that has been found by someone else and burned up by thousands. Maybe it's old age or maybe it's because I'm an ace dipper-outer (see glossary again). I've certainly nothing against twitchers or twitching, but it does seem to me that there is a tendency nowadays for young birders to start off rarity-hunting without first working on their knowledge of

common species. I feel we might well be seeing a new
generation of birders who would be hot enough on telling a
Raddes from a Dusky Warbler but would have a lot of
trouble sorting out a Marsh from Willow Tit or, more to the
point perhaps, could they honestly be sure about that Dusky
Warbler if they don't really know their Chiffchaffs?
Anyway, during my Bartley years I certainly got to see a few
Chiffchaffs and a few Willow Tits, though I don't think I ever
did see a Marsh Tit there. I certainly didn't see any Dusky
Warblers. Mind you, that only goes to prove my point. A
Marsh Tit would have been just as rare for Bartley as a Dusky
Warbler! (Be honest though, even then, I'd have preferred
the Dusky Warbler . . .)

Dusky Warbler, Raddes and Chiffchaff . . .
Identification is based simply on degrees of visibility . . . easy to see, quite
difficult to see, and impossible . . . so which is which?

At Bartley I also developed various birding skills. I learnt
how to use my ears as much as, or even sometimes more than,
my eyes: listening for those invisible waders flying over the
nasty concrete reservoir as fast as they could. And I learnt
how to 'read the weather'. Bartley was one of the last
Midland reservoirs to ice over, and so it was always worth a
visit during a really cold spell, when I could rack up a record
number of Tufted Duck when the wretched little things had
been frozen out of their usual cosy lakes and had had to turn
to Bartley as the last resort. A snowfall would usually provide
a 'weather movement', and I'd skid off on my bike to go
counting the Lapwings fleeing the country, always hoping to
cop for the odd Golden Plover with them. The birder's
friend, the east wind, could have its effect even on Bartley
and blow in a Black Tern or even a Little Gull – once! I also
learnt how to get up early – most of the best birds flew over
during the first two or three hours of daylight. And I learnt
the loneliness of the long-distance bird-watcher; and how to
beware of those dangerous days when optimism borders on
hallucination. My mind must have already been faltering as
early as 1956 when on 2 December I recorded a Flamingo at
ten o'clock, followed an hour later by an Eleonora's Falcon!
I'm happy to say that I'd calmed down by the time I wrote up
the event in my big notebook. By the evening the Flamingo
had been properly demoted:

'It must be an escape.'

The Falcon, mind you, nearly got through:

'It was black all over except for a possible fading on the
upper breast. Longish tail, never fanned, and typical Falcon
wings, although slightly wider perhaps. Colour, shape and
size comply only with Eleonora's Falcon.'

Then, thank God, I saw sense:

'. . . but since this bird has never been recorded in Britain,
it seems reasonable to suppose it was a melanistic variety;
probably a Kestrel.'

'Probably' indeed! Of course it was a bleeding Kestrel, you twit! However it *was* a *funny-looking* Kestrel, and the bird more than made up for not being new to the British list by reappearing on and off for the next three years and earning me those three sets of initials in the report.

Bartley taught me patience, and it taught me how to keep records. Not only did I have my notebooks and my prize essay and the two-part published survey, I also kept a dossier of every known notable bird ever recorded in the area. This I assembled by spending weeks in the Birmingham Reference Library searching through ancient reports and bulletins going back to 1931 when the Reservoir was constructed. Naturally these old records told of enviable glorious days gone by: a flock of no less than seventeen Dunlin in 1935; thirty Common Scoter after gales in October 1946; a party of four Velvet Scoter in 1947; a Spotted Crake, a Firecrest and even a Leach's Petrel in 1950. I'd have died for such birds! Still, there were consolations. As long ago as 1945 the records told of how the water bailiff was already bombarding Gulls (and I daresay farmers were going 'Oi!'). It was also comforting to note that way back in 1937, the then Bartley watcher had also started seeing Flamingoes! They'd tried to cover it up by claiming it had escaped from Dudley Zoo . . . but I knew better. It was nice to know others had suffered before me.

Another exciting day at Frankley Reservoir

If, as those past records suggested, Bartley in the fifties had gone off a bit since the forties, it had deteriorated even further by the start of the sixties. During the years I had been going there I had witnessed the insidious creeping encroachment of more housing estates and the destruction of rural habitat. On my first visit I'd noted a splendid old ramshackle farm, complete with resident Barn Owl. By my second visit it had been pulled down. Almost overnight three vast multistorey blocks of flats loomed up behind the meadow along the east side of the reservoir, constituting a serious flight hazard for migrating waders – if they looked down they'd crash right into them! Next came a curious mixed blessing. One of the local King Edward's Grammar Schools chose to remove its buildings and 800 boys from dilapidated premises near the centre of Birmingham to a vast new complex overlooking Bartley Reservoir. It was hardly what the conservationists would have ordered. On the other hand, the school contained several keen young birders including Andrew Lowe (the notorious ARL) who was at least able to keep a regular eye on the birds from his classroom window or whilst galloping around the rugby field. An unfair advantage, I always thought, when it came to chalking up initials!

Saddest of all, in September 1960, not only Bartley but the Midlands lost one of its most delightful bird spots – Westminster Farm was filled in. It's always bothered me that maybe the farmer, not content with clobbering me with my telescope, may have destroyed the habitat as his final act of revenge on trespassing schoolboy birders, in which case I have a lot to feel guilty about. Bartley is even more built up today. Nevertheless wandering wild-fowl and straying Gulls are amazingly oblivious to how ugly their temporary stopovers sometimes are, and migrants don't really seem to care what they fly over. If you are around the Midlands, Bartley is still worth a visit. Only a couple of years ago I spent a very pleasant evening as an invited guest at a meeting of the

West Midland Bird Club – the first one I'd ever attended! I couldn't resist browsing through the latest bulletin with news of recent good birds in the Midlands. Nostalgia provoked me to check the latest reports from my old patch. I suppose I was happy for some lucky birder, but I must have audibly sighed as I read of Glaucous and Iceland Gulls and all three species of Diver – all recorded at Bartley! Already that winter they'd had more good birds there in one month than I'd had in ten years!!

1. The friendly warning on the fence at Bartley.

2. The water bailiff and his furry chum. This photo was taken quite recently – the fencing has changed, but I do believe it's the same dog.

3. A dream come true – twenty years too late. Concrete mud exposed on the Bartley Shore, 1982. (Actually, even then there were only two Common Sandpipers and a bunch of gulls.)

4. Westminster Farm – before and after – a failure of conservation.

5
Branching out

Obsessed though my narrow young mind was with Bartley Reservoir I did occasionally stray further afield, though my range was necessarily restricted by available transport. I had become a teenager without the aid of a car, or, rather more to the point, my Dad was over forty before he acquired *his* first vehicle. Although Dad could hardly be described as a swinger, his first car was surprisingly racey. It was an MG. Most young men men tend to start their driving careers with a sports-car phase, and apparently late-starting middle-aged men go through it too. Dad must have been suitably embarrassed by his urge as he always claimed that his MG wasn't *really* a sports-car. True, it did have a roof and was therefore classed as a saloon, and it was a sober, if shiny, black. But it *was* an MG. Young blades in proper open-top MGs, complete with cavalry twill trousers, cravats and blondes in headscarves, used to flash their headlights at Dad, and he used to flash back in acknowlegement of their mutual member-ship of the MG 'club'. Dad's car shouldn't have qualified. I'd agree with him it wasn't *really* a sports-car. Being black and angular, it looked more like a small souped-up hearse, or an economy-sized gangster's get-away vehicle. Not that Dad ever drove very fast. In fact he drove very slowly.

But the important thing was he drove *me*. It must have been a very tedious chore for him, but quite often he used to save me the bike ride, take me to Bartley on a Sunday morning in the car, leave me there to do my rounds, and come back later and pick me up. It was probably boredom with doing this run that persuaded him to suggest I get a provisional driver's licence for myself. Bartley's lack of beauty and birds meant it was also free from people and traffic, and the road round the reservoir was an ideal place for learning to drive. About the only sign of life on a Sunday morning there was a gaggle of incompetent learners practising three-point turns. Dad no doubt reckoned he was doing himself a favour by teaching me. He must certainly have instructed me well. Immediately after my seventeenth birthday, I took my test and passed. From then on, most Sundays Dad let me borrow the MG to go off birding. He presumably decided that being relieved of giving me lifts was worth the worry of wondering if I was going to crash his car. He had reason to worry.

One wintry Sunday I set off at dawn, telling him I was, as usual, going off to Bartley. It was not true. Instead I drove off to my girlfriend's house. Well, I say 'girlfriend', but the fact was that though we had been stepping out together for ages we hadn't really done very much, if you know what I mean. We'd just about achieved 'number two' on the teenage sex ladder: 'holding hands', or was it *thinking about* holding hands'? It wasn't for want of my trying. Helen was a Catholic and a ballet dancer: a lethally repressive combination and as effective a deterrent to a young man's ardour as a bucket of cold water.

Anyway, coming up to one Sunday, she'd asked me if I'd be willing to drive her to London. Of course I immediately said yes. I saw this as a chance to please and impress, and perhaps qualify for a small carnal reward – being allowed to kiss her forehead perhaps. Later, on Saturday evening, she rang to warn me that any erotic intentions I might have had would be somewhat inhibited by the presence of . . . her mother. *She* needed a lift to London too. Her mother was also Catholic, with Jewish connections, and an opera singer and German. Altogether she was the ultimate weapon in the defence of a young girl's honour. Even then I lived in hope. Perhaps the idea was that I would drop Mum in London, then drive back with Helen, and we could pull into a secluded soft-verge off the M1 . . . and . . . hold hands? Yes? No. They *both* wanted to be dropped off in London, and I'd have to drive back alone. Oh what fun! Still, being a lad of my word, I couldn't back out and I agreed to do it. However, for some reason I didn't tell my Dad. Looking back on it, I'm sure the motive for my deceit was sheer embarrassment. I could not face admitting to my father that I was so wet as to have been conned into driving 200 miles, missing my day's bird-watching and not even getting a naughty nibble at the end of it. I'd figured my shame would never be discovered.

Dad was used to me being out all day on Sunday: the time it took me to do Bartley – or get to London and back. So that Sunday I set off at dawn as was my wont, telling my Dad I was off birding. I had to waste four hours dozing in a side street before the appointed time for picking up Helen and her mother. The drive down to London was every bit as thrilling and picturesque as a trip down a concrete motorway usually is. Nobody spoke much. However, the tedium was a little relieved by the fact that I had to call in every services from Birmingham to Watford Gap. The little orange light kept coming on and I had to keep filling up with oil. If I *did* fill up, the little orange light went out for at least ten minutes, then it came on again, and I'd stop again and find the oil needed another two or three pints. This went on all the way down to

London. People with a more sophisticated knowledge of cars than I had then (or have now, for that matter) would have suspected that something was wrong. I reckon Helen and her mother both had an idea all was not well. As soon as we reached London they raced away from the car as if it were about to blow up. I set off back northwards, my anxious little face again lit up by the cheerful glow of the oil warning light. After a while the engine started making nasty clanking noises. I was pleased when these soon faded and the car went delightfully quiet. I was not so pleased when I realised that this was because it had stopped working altogether. Silently and gracefully I free-wheeled across the path of three juggernauts (I think I went under the third one), glided across the hard shoulder and came to rest halfway up a grass bank. An hour or so later I had to make a slightly embarrassing phone call:

'Er, Dad . . . you're not going to believe this . . . but . . . listen . . . I didn't go bird-watching . . . I took Helen and her mother . . . yes, I said her mother . . . I took them to the station . . . no, not New Street . . . King's Cross . . . yes . . . so, actually, I'm not at the reservoir . . . I'm in Newport Pagnell . . . and I'm calling because . . . yes, the car *has* broken down . . . well, I'm not sure exactly what it means but the man at the garage says the big end's gone.'

Dad had to get a new car. This was an enormous Ford Zephyr 6 capable of doing 100 m.p.h. as I discovered tazzing down the motorway on the way to the Wild Fowl Trust at Slimbridge on another Sunday when I'd told Dad I was just nipping off to Bartley. Yes, amazingly he didn't hold the big-end affair against me. He *still* let me borrow his car. It was technically a 'firm' car – part of Dad's promotion package at the West Midlands Electricity Board – so maybe he didn't care so much what happened to it. Actually nothing ever *did*, except he must have sometimes wondered if there was something wrong with the mileometer as the Bartley run could rack anything between ten and a hundred miles. So where did I drive in his enormous Zephyr? Well, no birder could live on Bartley alone and, as an avid reader of the West Midland Bird Reports, I could hardly ignore the fact that other people's initials appeared on other reservoirs. Nor that the birds recorded there were pretty tempting. Inside the copy of the 1957 report I had compiled a list of twenty-three desirable Midlands locations with map references and a one to five star rating system, on which, incidentally, Bartley scored three stars. Mind you, this apparently impressive rating is put more into perspective by the fact that seven waters scored four or five stars and most of the one- and two-star places were really naff little park ponds and boating pools. Nevertheless, the exercise did reassure me that statistically Bartley was by no means the *worst* place in the Midlands, and there may well have been other bird-watchers suffering more than me. On the other hand, there were people out there enjoying themselves and seeing a lot more birds and, even back in 1957 – two years before my motorisation – that list was proof that I was already hankering a little for reservoirs new.

With the coming of my Dad's motorcar and my seventeenth birthday I got my chance to branch out. Incidentally, I should perhaps explain the obsession with reservoirs. Quite simply, to the land-locked birders of Birmingham, seventy miles or so from the nearest sea, reservoirs are by far the richest focal point for a variety of bird life and the only places where the population is at all unpredictable. You *can* watch birds in woodlands and meadows of course, and very nice too, but go there week after week and you tend to keep seeing the same things. In the Midlands the summer migrants tend to arrive at their nesting places, breed and go away again. Delightful, but predictable. In winter they may be replaced by foraging parties of Tits or flocks of Buntings or winter Thrushes. Again a lovely sight, but not a lot of variety. With patience, imagination and enterprise a bird watcher may well turn this comparative sameness into an advantage and concentrate on behaviour studies or breeding population surveys and so on. Arguably this is more valuable to the science of ornithology than hunting for rare birds. Nevertheless to most birders their hobby is not a science but a game, albeit an obsessive and indeed educational one. I know that when I skimmed through the pages of a newly arrived annual report I was looking for 'Leach's Petrel at Cannock' rather than 'Sixteen pairs of Coal Tits bred in Wyre Forest this year'. To be honest, I'd rather have been at the reservoir than in the wood, and I am pretty sure most Birmingham birders would have been with me.

I suppose the reservoirs are first and foremost seaside substitutes or counterfeit estuaries. There are Gulls and wildfowl and, if the shoreline is muddy, there will be Waders. The population is somehow more glamorous and more fluctuating, and rarities are comparatively frequent. There's always a chance of a Diver or the scarcer Grebes or Terns or a good Wader. True, now and again the wood-watchers get lucky, and when they do it's often a 'crippler'. I recall reading of Midlands records of a Black-throated Thrush being pulled out of a mist-net full of winter buntings, and a Pallas's Warbler from a catch of Goldcrests, and a Dusky Thrush coming to feed on a Worcestershire compost heap. But such events are, to say the least, infrequent and the chances of you or me being there to enjoy them are positively remote. Reservoir watchers are much less likely to dip out. For a start the watery rarities tend to be bigger and easier to see, floating on the water or flapping over it or feeding on the mud. Anyway reservoirs seem to attract many of the best 'little birds' as well. Spring migrants always seem to fall and concentrate around the reservoirs when they arrive in the Midlands, before they disperse to their breeding habitats, and in autumn there is quite a lot of evidence to suggest that birds use the reservoirs, and the river valleys in which they often lie, as visible orientation marks on their migration routes. After bad weather, concentrations of small birds can often be found refuelling in the reeds and willows round the Midlands reservoirs, much as they would do on a coastal promontory or on an island. It's no wonder really then that when it comes to luring the inland birder reservoirs have it.

Even on my bike I had occasionally strayed from Bartley's concrete shores. Now that I was able to nab Dad's car it was impossible to resist such excursions. It was a dangerous tendency because I couldn't help making comparisons with my home patch. The most immediate available comparison was about half an hour's drive away, Bittell Reservoirs. They are in Worcestershire about five miles from Redditch and about a mile from the rather comically named Lickey Hills; so called, I suspect, because at week-ends they attract thousands of young Brummies licking either ice-creams or each other. The Lickeys are mainly pine forest and larches providing excellent cover for Siskins, Redpolls and courting couples. As a beginner I had occasionally been to 'Bittell Resers' (as I knew them) on the bus. I caught a Number 63 from outside my school, got off at the Lickeys and then had to walk rather a long way. All a bit of a bore. Or, now and then, I'd cycle from Bartley. This was not bad on the way there – a long free-wheel down from Frankley Beaches and another one down from the Lickeys. On the way back, I had to get off and push most of the way. All a bit harrowing. In the car it was a doddle to Bittell; and it was good value there. There are three stretches of water. Lower Bittell is very pleasant, a natural-looking lake with grassy banks, areas of reeds and lilies. There were always lots of wild-fowl there, though rarities were, perhaps surprisingly, not that frequent. But it was pretty good for Terns and early migrants in spring. It was also easy to look at from the road, which went most of the way round it, and through a hedge that had had several

little square gaps cut out of it especially for leaning telescopes
on. On the other side of this road was a small pool called Mill
Shrub; also very pleasant and often more productive than the
bigger reservoir. This is often the way. It's extraordinary how
many British reservoirs have a little bit cut off by the road or a
bridge that tends to be favoured by the better birds. There's
one at Abberton Reservoir in Essex, at Stithians in Cornwall
and at Chew near Bristol. Or maybe it's just that rare birds
are easier to spot on little pools than out in the middle of
whacking great reservoirs! Anyway, Mill Shrub was often
good for a rare Grebe in winter or the first Garganey in late
March. After checking Lower Bittell and Mill Shrub I would
drive – probably illegally – up a cart track and park near a
farm, hop over a stile, on what I *think* was a public right of
way, and emerge on the grassy-topped dam of Upper Bittell.

Rare birds may well prefer squitty little ponds to attractive
big lakes, but they are even more partial to really nasty places.
Upper Bittell could be really appalling. Not that it's
particularly unsightly. It's quite a large area of water and
nearly a mile across. There are no reeds or lilies and along one
side the shoreline is of a weird copper-coloured flakey cross
between mud and shale that sticks to your shoes and repels
birds. Probably it sticks to their feet and beaks too. However,
the rest of the banks are of low, rough grass and would be
perfectly presentable if they didn't attract the overspill from
the nearby Lickeys. At weekends the shores of Upper Bittell
could look like Brighton Beach on a bank holiday, except
that half of the day-trippers were armed, either with air rifles
or dogs or both. On such days it was no place for the timid
birder. There was a nice little muddy stretch of shoreline as
well, but this was barricaded by barbed wire as it belonged
inevitably to the yacht club. If I ever let my wellie accidently
hop over into that forbidden territory I'd soon be chased off
by a chorus of nautical 'Ois!' from gentlemen in blue
blazers and sailor caps. Having drunk their morning rum, or

whatever yachtsmen have for breakfast, they would slip into their bright orange bird-scaring jackets, splice their main-braces, and career round the reservoir chasing the Ducks off the water. If the birds landed on the shore they'd be shot at by cowboys or pounced on by Alsatians. Yet, nasty though it could be, Upper Bittell often had the rarest birds; and what's more, *I* saw some of them! The secret was to get there really early in the morning, or in mid-week during school holidays, and especially when, through some lucky piece of mis-management by the Water Board, the water-level had been dropped low enough to expose vast areas of squelching muddy shoreline, thus engulfing the day trippers and screwing up the yachtsmen but attracting the Waders.

Upper Bittell was a place of contrasts. It could be lousy or it could be great. 24 May 1959 my notebook records grumpily:

'No birds: "N" hundred Teds and Freds.'

But on 10 December 1961 I got out before them *and* the water was low . . . my notebook tells a different tale:

'One Redshank, one Adult Kittiwake, one Snow Bunting

(all good Midlands birds) and one Kite. A bird flew quite low south-east to north-west mobbed by Crows. Red tail, brown plumage, pale braces, deeply forked tail etc all clearly noted.' The first Midland record for over ten years.

The three Bittell Reservoirs actually offered quite a nice balance for a day's birding. Always numbers of birds at Lower Bittell, usually something nice on Mill Shrub and the total unpredictability of Upper Bittell. All in all, I had to own up it tended to put Bartley in its place. The comparison was unavoidable and a teeny bit odious:

'1959 December 27th. Bittell: 380 Mallard 220 Teal, 77 Wigeon, 17 Tufted, 6 Pochard and a Pintail.'

'Bartley: 1 Dabchick.'

Yet I never entirely deserted Bartley. Now motorised, I would do Bartley in the very early morning, drive over and do Bittell in the still fairly early morning and get back to Bartley for the afternoon. It was this routine that revealed a curious and profitable relationship between the two reservoirs. On 8 November 1959 I was about to leave Bartley at 10 o'clock when sixteen Wigeon and twenty-three Mallard landed on the water. Such numbers were so rare an event there that I thought things couldn't possibly get any better and, well satisfied, I set off for Bittell. At quarter to twelve I was up at Upper Bittell and, being fairly late, it was predictably well down to its worst form – no Ducks at all. So I drove back to Bartley and, as I arrived, so did fifteen Pochard, five Tufted and twenty-four more Mallard, making an almost record breaking total of fifty-six Mallard. My suspicions were aroused, and two Sundays later I was able to follow up my theory. Early morning at Bartley was bleak and birdless. Off I drove to Bittell with Andrew Lowe. Between the two main reservoirs there was the usual large number of wild-fowl, including a flock of thirty-five Wigeon and, a rare sight for the Midlands, a party of nine Cormorants. Then the Teds and Freds arrived and the yachtsmen launched their attack. My notebook records: 'All the Duck were flying when we left.' We raced back to Bartley. Ninety-two Mallard beat us to it. A few minutes later exactly thirty-five Wigeon flew in and, to complete the transfer, we looked up to see nine Cormorants circling overhead. The theory was proved. Such was my loyalty to Bartley that, from then on, I regarded my visits to Bittell as being largely for the purpose of swelling the Bartley totals for the National Wild-fowl Counts which took place one Sunday each month. Usually the Teds and Freds, yacht club or even West Midland Bird Club field meetings would do the job for us. But if nothing had arrived by twelve o'clock, we were certainly not beyond nipping over and giving the Ducks a gentle push in the right direction; though we only resorted to these unsporting tactics on Wild-fowl Count days.

1960 was a particularly good year for unprovoked transfers, when over fifty Pochard and up to seventy Wigeon arrived at Bartley regularly each Sunday just after lunch, without us ever having to go and get them. But these numbers were eclipsed by the record invasions of 1961. I don't know what was going on at Bittell that winter but the Ducks must have hated it, and Bartley certainly benefited.

The year began – 1 January 1961 – with a wonderous avalanche of seventy Mallard, sixty-eight Wigeon, eight Teal, fifty-eight Tufted and 187 Pochard. Whatever was upsetting them at Bittell obviously didn't happen on 6 January. Nothing arrived, and we were right down to the true Bartley population – a Tufted Duck and a Dabchick. So two days later we went to get them again. We persuaded ninety Mallard and 220 Pochard to make the crossing. I returned to university after my Christmas holiday satisfied that I was the new holder of the official Bartley Pochard record. Three weeks later I heard that Andrew Lowe had decided to challenge me. He didn't have a car but, knowing his competitive spirit, he probably ran to Upper Bittell and swam around waving a red flag. Anyway, it worked. 29 January: a new Bartley record of 150 Tufted and 260 Pochard – both ARL. My crown was slipping. I was being usurped by these uppety youngsters! Clearly I needed to find another patch. Later in 1961 I found it.

Whilst doing the research for my momentous two-part work on the birds of Bartley Reservoir I had spent many hours in the Reference Library looking back through those old reports. My eyes had often strayed to the records from other Midlands locations. Most of them were places I knew, that were being well watched, and indeed, in Dad's Zephyr, I'd even visited some of them. If I set out early enough I could do a West Midlands circuit that took in all seven of the four- or five-star reservoirs. I'd always start out at Bartley but give it a less than usually thorough scrutiny – say, two minutes – just time to count the Dabchick. Then I'd set off on my expedition. The main part of the run was the A5 reservoirs in Staffordshire. There were three waters along this dead straight ex-Roman road. At the western end came Belvide which, even in my younger days, had a proper hide, a fair indication that there were birds to be watched from it – not that *I* ever saw anything that good there. Then there was Gailey Reservoir: actually two adjacent large square areas of water that looked as if they belonged in the grounds of a stately home. There was a wooded island in the middle with half-dead trees on it that might have been designed for Ospreys. All I ever saw on it was Cormorants – there was a strange inland colony living there. I once found a Ferruginous Duck at Gailey. It was an important bird for me as I think my report was regarded as the inaccurate ravings of an over-optimistic youngster by the then secretary of the West Midland Bird Club until his curiosity got the better of him and he went to have a look for himself. He found I was right. It *was* a Ferruginous, and no doubt a tick for *him* too. After that I was generally believed. After Gailey, at the eastern end of the A5, came Cannock Reservoir, or Chase Water. This was Upper Bittell with knobs on. It was often a nightmare. It had only a yacht club but, God help us, an aqua-sports centre, complete with water skiers and speed boats. It was also surrounded by slag heaps. But, true to the rare bird-nasty place theory, Cannock regularly turned up the Midlands most stunning rarities. This hideous place obviously has some God-given ornithological connections with Scotland, the Mediterranean and eastern Canada. The slag heaps have a resident winter flock of Twite, and its star rarities over recent years have included Red-footed Falcon, Lesser Kestrel, Buff-breasted and Least Sandpiper, and the only inland British record of Cory's Shearwater. Even *I* saw a Leach's Petrel there once. Cutting up north from Cannock I would end up at what is probably the most impressive of all Midlands reservoirs – Blithfield.

My first visit, in August 1961, was a dreadful shock to my system. I was still in the habit of lying for hours on my back at Bartley hoping to hear a Dunlin. Blithfield was rather better than that. 23 August 1961:

'75 Ringed Plover, 30 Dunlin, 20 Redshank, 5 Common Sandpipers, 5 Green Sandpipers, 2 Wood Sandpipers, 25 Ruff, 9 Greenshank, 6 Turnstone, 3 Dusky Redshank, 1 Black Tailed Godwit.'

Assuming the whole thing was an hallucination, I went back a week later to make sure I was dreaming and added eleven Whimbrel, two Little Stints, sixteen Common Terns, six Little Terns and a Little Gull. Clearly Blithfield was *not* the place I was looking for! Such numbers could hardly remain a secret and indeed as surely as I saw Waders there, I also saw other bird-watchers. The same was true of Belvide and Gailey and even the extraordinary Cannock. They were all too well known. As a new local patch they were useless. What I was looking for was somewhere yet undiscovered or

perhaps somewhere that had been forgotten. As I researched
the earliest days of Bartley's history I sorted through moth-
eaten, dog-eared bird club reports from the 1930s and came
across a location I hadn't heard of before – Upton Warren.
There were pre-war records of Long-tailed Duck and Scoter,
so it must have been a lake or a reservoir of some sort, yet the
name didn't ring a bell. It hadn't figured at all on my twenty-
three Midland Bird Spots League Table. Perhaps it was a
pool that had been filled in during the war, or maybe
somehow it had just been forgotten. I got the one-inch map,
Ordnance Survey number 130, published 1954, fully revised
1949, with corrections to 1957. There it was, Upton Warren
– a little village between Bromsgrove and Droitwich, and
not a splash of blue anywhere near it. No water marked. If
there ever was any there it must have been filled in long ago.
Then I got my latest Bird Club Bulletin and read: 'Little
Grebe: maximum of 30 at Upton Warren.' Not a record to
set the birders twitching but there obviously *was* something
there. Thirty Dabchicks wouldn't just sit out in the middle of
a field. They prefer water. Whatever Upton Warren was, it
still existed. On 14 January 1961 I went there and found it.

There seemed to be two areas of water. One was a fairly
small square gravel pit with a few little islands on it; the banks
were steep and not at all suitable for waders, it was the
headquarters of – guess what? – a yacht club! No birds could
surely stay on there for long without disturbance. That day
there weren't any. Perhaps they'd flown off to Bartley.
Actually they didn't have to go that far. A few hundred yards
away was a second pool and it looked rather interesting. It
was on farm-land, far enough away from the road to be
undisturbed. It looked almost like subsidence flooding and
may well have been. There were several dead tree trunks, half
submerged, and the water was obviously only a few feet
deep. At the end of winter it was probably swollen by rainfall
and I remember thinking that if it dried up later in the year it

could well expose some nice muddy edges, or maybe it would just disappear altogether. I christened this the 'flood meadow'. Perhaps this was where the Dabchicks had been. There weren't any that day, but there *were* other birds. Not a spectacular gathering, but enough to be encouraging:

'20 Teal, 12 Tufted, 6 Pochard, 2 Wigeon and 15 Coot.'

From 1960 to 1963 I was at Cambridge University and I only went back to Birmingham during the holidays. I was increasingly beginning to take bird trips to the remoter parts of Britain, so my Midlands watching was steadily decreasing. I was also still a Bartley regular. Nevertheless, I kept popping back over to Upton. It hardly ever failed to turn up something interesting. On 8 April 1961 the first Wader – a Dunlin. In July I found Redshank breeding there, along with Tufted Ducks and Yellow Wagtails. Later that month a Green Sandpiper and another Dunlin. In the winter of 1962–63 it was mainly frozen over, but still managed to produce a Golden-eye, two Pintail and up to sixty Teal. 15 March 1963 there was a delightful contrast: the first two Garganey of the year on the flood meadow and a Great Northern Diver on the gravel pit. A week later the Diver had been joined by two Bewick's Swans. On comparatively few visits I'd already accumulated quite a nice list of species and so far I'd only met one other bird-watcher, apart from Andrew Lowe who often came with me. Upton Warren was obviously not bad at all. But it was actually better than I then knew. As it turned out, it was Bewick's Swans again which showed me its full potential. The date was 15 December 1963. I had in fact been to Upton the day before and had a White-fronted Goose and a wintering Ruff on the flood meadow. Encouraged, I returned with Andrew on the 14th and was disappointed to find neither of yesterday's birds visible. It was rather cold, overcast and with a light drizzle, and we resolved to set off on an A5 reservoir run. As we got back to the car we heard the plaintive honking of wild swans approaching out of the mist. A family party of Bewicks circled above us: two adults and four juveniles. We expected them to pitch down on the gravel pit, but they didn't. Instead they flew straight across the water, still quite high. Presumably they were going to go straight through without stopping. But no, they began to loose height and about a hundred yards beyond the pit they dipped behind a tall hawthorn hedge and disappeared out of view. They didn't reappear. As far as we could tell they had crash-landed in a dry field! Bewick's Swans are worth a second look at any time and in the Midlands doubly so. So we clambered over the yacht club gate, hurried along the side of the pit and scrambled towards the hawthorn hedge. Cautiously we peeped through. What we saw was like a little corner of the Ouse Washes. The area the swans had landed in was not at all visible from the road or from any point on our usual Upton route. It wasn't a dry field at all. There were the swans, feeding busily along the side of another shallow pool, and between us and them was another one, with muddy edges and short stubbly reeds, and then, beyond the birds, was a third small area of water with a respectable growth of taller reeds. It was a superb habitat. It must have looked good to the swans, and surely to Waders, and definitely to bird-watchers – only at that time nobody seemed to know it was there, except us. Clearly Upton Warren was to be my new local patch. The pity of it was I hadn't discovered it years ago.

By the end of 1963 I was already working in the West End theatre. The 1963 Cambridge Footlights Revue, *Cambridge Circus*, had successfully transferred to London and I was living in Paddington – a bit too far to nip over to Upton each Sunday. My Dad tried to co-operate by moving from the semi in Oak Tree Crescent to a flat on a new estate at Hagley, and from there it was only a twenty-minute drive to Upton. Whenever I did visit the Midlands to see Dad I would nip off to my new favourite haunt. Alas, my work continued to get in the way of more important things. In summer of 1964 *Cambridge Circus* flew off to New Zealand and from there to New York, where we jolly varsity pranksters became the toast of Broadway. Well, actually we closed after three weeks, but we moved into a smaller theatre and then traipsed all over America doing shows on university campuses. The result of that is I *still* have a longer list of American birds than British, but that's another story and another book.

Meanwhile, back in the swinging sixties. Despite the lure of Hollywood my heart was still at Upton Warren. The roar of the greasepaint could never drown the 'chiff-if-if' of a Wood Sandpiper. 9 May 1965, two days after returning from the States, that was exactly what I was enjoying – 'One Wood Sandpiper along with two Blue-headed Wagtails and Ring Ouzel.' The wonder of it was that news of Upton's potential still hadn't really spread to other Birmingham birders and though it wasn't being entirely neglected, it certainly wasn't being covered as well as it deserved.

I was determined to make up for my lost year and I drew up a plan of the Upton area in my notebook. The 'Bewick's fields' were now designated the 'flood meadows', whilst the original marshy pool had become the 'main pool'. The gravel pit remained the 'Pit'. I always knew those shallow little flashes would eventually produce good Waders and, on 12 May 1965, they did. My brain must have still been in New York. When I spotted two small warm-brown scaley-plumaged 'peeps' with yellow legs, my commentary immediately identified them as Least Sandpipers. A few minutes later I realised I was back in Worcestershire. Of course they weren't *that* good, but what I *had* got was a pair of Temminck's Stints in their delightful breeding colours. A very rare occurrence fifteen miles from Birmingham city centre, and Upton's best bird so far.

During the rest of 1965 I got off to see Dad or rather, be honest, Upton Warren, as often as I could. I was now fully mobile with my very own grotty little dark brown Vauxhall Viva, a strange oblong vehicle that looked like a large Mars bar on wheels. Andrew Lowe had also matured to the point of passing his driving test and, true to form, had set himself to carry on my good work. Between us and the occasional enlightened outside visitor, we gave Upton a thorough going-over that autumn. The West Midland Bird Report 1965 tells the tale. By the end of the year Upton had recorded twenty-three species of Waders, including a Red-necked Phalarope, along with four species of Terns. A tiny place with a big rating. Definitely five stars. And now the news was out! Naturally more and more birders began to call in at Upton. Better coverage brought even better birds. In March 1968 Upton Warren had its first proper real national rarity, and I thought I'd found it. It was 17 March and my notebook records the possibly significant weather details:

'Wind: west-south-west force 8, after several days westerly gales.'

I hadn't been to Upton for nearly six months and it was nice to be back. Most of the birds were on the main flood. As I approached it a few Snipe zipped out, along with a couple of yelping Redshank. There was a nice mixed flotilla of wildfowl out on the water, including a pair of Pintail. My commentary was optimistic:

'Mm . . . looking good for the spring's first Garganey . . . and there it is . . . no it isn't . . . what the hell's that?'

There was a small duck dabbling tantalisingly amongst the vegetation at the edge of the lake. A touch of blue grey and a flash of white crescent − but it *wasn't* a Garganey. My immediate thought was it must be an exotic escape from the Wild-Fowl Trust Collection at Slimbridge. Then I realised I'd seen one of these before. In fact I'd seen half a dozen, in late April 1965 . . . at Jamaica Bay Wild Life Refuge, New York. It was male American Blue-winged Teal. I scribbled a sketch and took notes enough to convince any rarities committee. Then the moment of truth. I walked closer, trying to suppress my fear that the bird would come quacking over to me to be fed. Almost to my relief, it was the first Duck to fly off, even before the notoriously wary Teal. My notebook echoes my sigh of satisfaction:

'The bird was very wild, and took flight before the accompanying Teal. It flew strongly with no signs of wing clipping; also no ring was noted on the legs, which were conspicuous due to their colour (orange). *British Birds* states that: "The bird is very rarely kept in captivity and considering its rarity and value is unlikely to be allowed to escape." Other points to a genuine bird − there have been westerly gales for the past week. Also this species would be on the

move at this time of the year up the Atlantic coast of the
States.'

The authorities agreed with me, and *British Birds* 'Report
on Rare Birds in Great Britain in 1968' records the event:

Blue Winged Teal *Anas discors.*
   Worcestershire, Upton Warren. ♂ , 11th to 27th of March (A.F. Jacobs,
   J. Lord, B.T. Nichols *et al*).

'Et al'! – that was me I suppose. I *hadn't* found it at all!
Apparently it had arrived at Upton about a week before I
had, but for some reason the news hadn't spread. I recall
ringing up the secretary of the bird club on the evening of the
17th, and he hadn't heard of it then. Maybe the original
finder had decided to suppress it for fear of an invasion of
twitchers (not likely in those days) or maybe he hadn't been
able to believe his own eyes till somebody else confirmed it. It
doesn't matter. It was a beautiful little Duck – or rather
Drake – and it stayed long enough to be enjoyed by many
Midlands birders. It also guaranteed even more attention for
Upton Warren.

Later that same year another real rarity turned up. 7
October, a Richard's Pipit – frequent enough on the Scillies
perhaps, but not near Droitwich! Since then Upton has
notched up a pretty extraordinary score of excellent birds:
three Pectoral Sandpipers, up to six Temminck's Stints
together, White-winged Black and Caspian Tern, Black-
winged Stilt, Alpine Swift and another couple of Blue-
winged Teal! It has also become one of the most intensely
watched spots in the Midlands. The area has been bought and
managed by the Worcestershire Nature Conservation Trust
and is superbly laid out with trails and several hides. Water-
levels are controlled and the bird life is truly prolific.

I last visited it on 1 May 1978 when I took a party from the
RSPB Young Ornithologists Club on a guided tour of my
old haunt. It was well up to form: fourteen Dunlin, four

Ringed Plover, two Little Ringed Plover, Green and Common Sandpipers and Sanderling, Common Terns, Ruddy Duck and Shelduck and a couple of Blue-headed Wagtails. I confess I felt rather proud at the idea that I might have been one of the people who, over fifteen years before, had been involved in putting Upton on the map. Perhaps in a way I had helped to create this reserve which was now giving such pleasure to so many birders.

On the other hand, I had to admit I also felt a little sad. I remembered Upton in the early sixties – my very favourite kind of birding area. Three different types of habitat, all hidden from each other. If there was nothing on the gravel pit, there was always hope of something on the main pool and, if that failed me, there was bound to be a Wader or two hidden over the back flood fields. It took time to do it properly, yet it wasn't a large area. Nothing was ever so far away that I couldn't identify it, yet if I didn't cover every little corner of mud and marsh I could easily miss something. Birds came and went. A Tern might fly over at dawn and be gone, and new Waders would drop in at dusk. It was a full day's work, yet wonderfully manageable, constantly surprising and utterly unpredictable. It's still like that, but back in those days there were no nature trails, hides or information boards and virtually no other birders. I'll be honest, *that's* how I prefer to remember it. The ideal local patch. I wonder if nowadays there are any left in Britain? If you are aware of one, do please let me know – on the other hand, perhaps you shouldn't. Difficult decision, isn't it? After all, if Upton Warren hadn't become so popular, maybe it would have gone the way of Westminster Farm and been filled in. It seems these days that as much as bird-watchers need birds, the birds may need the bird-watchers.

On 4 June 1969 my regular Midland bird-watching came to an end at Upton Warren. Later that year my father died and I had no longer a reason to drive up to Birmingham. As

long as I could remember, Dad had suffered from bronchial
asthma. For years he'd made relatively light of it, referring to
the little inhaler he had to use as his 'puffer'. Whilst I lived at
home he never seemed to take his illness too seriously and
consequently neither did I. I remember he used to be gripped
by awful coughing fits and wheezy breathlessness. But a
couple of puffs seemed to put him right. I don't think he
wanted me to know how ill he was. He was extremely self-
conscious about the idea of his becoming a burden to me, and
he was determined that I would never have to look after him.
I feel sure this was the result of his having chosen to care for
his mother, my Granny. He had allowed her to dominate his
life and suppress his social life completely. When she died I
suppose, frankly, it must have been a relief to him. In a way it
gave him his freedom, but it was too late. During those years
he had got out of the habit of really being able to enjoy
himself. The presence of my Granny hardly allowed him to. I
think he knew it, and he had unselfishly resolved that I would
not be suppressed in the same way by him. In fact he took his
greatest pleasures in *my* achievements, many of which he
himself engineered. He made sure I went to the high school
and he guided me towards Cambridge. He took a dignified
pride in my egomaniacal exploits on the sportsfield at school
and on the stage at university. Afterwards he kept scrapbooks
full of my newspaper cuttings from the *Birmingham Post* to
the *New York Times*; from my scoring a try in the Public
School Seven-a-sides; to getting one of my jokes performed
by David Frost on *That Was The Week That Was*. He kept all
my school reports in a neatly bound file. When I won the
Natural History Prize he was delighted; when I failed French
'O' level he was almost in tears. Fortunately I made up for it
by getting an A+ in English. I hope it doesn't seem too
arrogant if I say I'm glad I was able to fulfil most of his
ambitions and I am genuinely very, very grateful indeed to
my Dad for the encouragement he gave me. He was a very

intelligent, modest and, above all, unselfish man. I wish for his sake he hadn't been.

Once I'd left home and moved to London he seemed to lose much of his enthusiasm and optimism, I shall never forget suddenly realising that, only a year or two after leaving university, I was actually earning more than my Dad. It must have seemed strange to him too. By the late sixties I had performed in the West End and on Broadway. I was an integral part of a hit radio series (*I'm Sorry I'll Read That Again*) and I was writing regularly for television. I'd also got married. As much as Dad took pride and joy in my success, it must also have drained him. It was as if his work was at an end. The bronchial asthma took over, almost as if he could now let it. He refused to come to London and live with me. He talked about my Granny and laughed about the awful Christmasses and the mess in the front room. I had told him it obviously wouldn't be like that with him, but I suppose I knew what he was saying. In 1968 he moved, alone, into a smaller flat and he was forced to retire from his job. In the summer of 1969 he went into hospital, and in the autumn he died.

Dad had no hobbies. He always claimed he didn't have time, which obviously wasn't true. The irony was that he devoted quite a lot of time to encouraging *my* hobby. He'd given me lifts to and from Bartley, he drove me around Norfolk on my first bird holiday at Cley and Blakeney. He'd lent me his car whenever he could so I could go bird-watching. He had no interest in birds and he never attempted to develop any. I've always wished he had done. I shall never know, maybe the asthma would have beaten him anyway, but I can't help feeling that if Dad had had *any* obsessional enthusiasm – be it bird-watching, stamp collecting or bee-keeping – he would not have died so young. I do know that I am greatly indebted to him for encouraging *my* obsession with birds. I honestly feel that some day it may save my life.

Birders talk about their 'life list', and that seems to me to be rather appropriate. A life list has no end. It can never be too long. I know I'll never live long enough to see everything I want to see . . . but I'm certainly going to try! For that, and so much else, thank you Dad.

1. Lower Bittell.

2. Upper Bittell, the Yacht Club – members are inside the clubhouse enjoying a drink after a hard morning's bird scaring.

3. Blithfield – doing a passable impression of the Camargue

1. Upton Warren in the early sixties. **2.** Upton today – a sign of progress . . . (the hide). **3.** Another sign of progress – this one belonging to the Worcestershire Conservation Trust . . . The 'Bewicks' pools in the background. **4.** And a sign of co-operation – almost unique – Upton Warren Sailing Centre and Nature Reserve – so it *isn't* a contradiction in terms! **5.** Blue-winged Teal (from Notebook) . . .

6
Observatories

Meanwhile back in the mid-fifties . . . new, older and more experienced birdy chums in the King Edward's School Natural History Society not only told me how to join the West Midland Bird Club and what bus to get to Belvide Reservoir – they also made me jealous. At the end of each school holiday we'd exchange recent reports and news. Mine would involve a couple of 'Comic Terns at Bartley Reservoir', whilst theirs would feature birds I'd hardly even heard of, let alone seen – Tawnies and Richard's (Pipits), Great and Lesser Greys (Shrikes), and always lots of Blue-throats and Wrynecks. All seen at faraway places with strange-sounding names, 'Dunge', 'Cley' and 'The Bill'. I'd slope off suitably impressed and look up the birds in my field guide. I wrote out a list of rare birds I'd like to see sometime. It included plenty of real rarities and plenty of more modest ambitions, headed by Red-backed Shrike, Wryneck and Blue-throat. I also compiled a second list: 'places I must try to visit'. One of my more helpful mates kindly acted as translator. 'Dunge' was Dungeness in Kent; 'the Bill' was probably Portland in Dorset but could also be Selsey in Sussex; and Cley was in north Norfolk. It was pronounced 'Cl-eye' not 'Clay', and actually referred to Blakeney Point. It was all a bit boggling but became clear enough in the fullness of time.

The point was, I was told, that all these places were bird observatories, and there were several others dotted around the coasts and islands of Britain. So I bought a big map and marked on it all the British bird observatories, along with a few other famous bird spots, such as the Wild Fowl Trust and the A5 reservoirs. So it was that in the mid-fifties I began a crusade I happily continue today: to work my way slowly round all the bird observatories in the British Isles. It's a slow process, as I tend to get addicted to particular favourites and return to them year after year, so there's still plenty I haven't yet visited; but that's something to look forward to and another incentive to live to a ripe old age.

I love bird observatories. However, my most vivid memory of a schoolboy observatory holiday from the mid-fifties is of a week spent at Dungeness in September 1957. It was a nightmare. By that time I was already in the habit of keeping a pretty elaborate notebook, yet my entry for my first visit to Dunge consists of *one* page covering *one* afternoon of *one* day. I've clearly tried to blank the rest of the visit out of my memory. So what horrible events took place on the missing six days? At the risk of reviving some dangerously traumatic teenage experience, I'll try to recall what happened. The mental pictures are disjointed yet scary – a bit like a Hitchcock horror movie!

There were three of us, I think, who set off from Birmingham one day in late August 1957. I presume we took a train to London and then caught another one that took us into deepest Kent. As we travelled further south-east more and more passengers got off the train until we were the only ones left. I remember looking out of the window. The train was entering a wasteland, a strange desolate landscape that looked like a vision of earth after a nuclear holocaust. There were miles of flat shingle dotted with sparse spikey shrubs, the carcasses of rusting vehicles and the skeletons of a few charred and collapsing buildings. It was clearly a forbidden zone. There were barricades of barbed wire and red flags flying, presumably warning of unexploded bombs or imminent gunfire. The train stopped at the very last station. The end of line. It went no further. We got out. The engine backed away over the horizon, as if in fear, and we were left alone on the tiny concrete platform, cringing under the weight of our enormous haversacks. I must have been given some secret instructions, because somehow I knew which direction to take. Under a merciless afternoon sun we trudged across the shingly wilderness for hours and hours, frequently falling down hidden rabbit holes or keeling over into gorse bushes. Suddenly we saw ahead of us what was surely a mirage. Shimmering through the heat haze in the middle of a desert – a lighthouse! We literally crawled closer, threading our way through a maze of strange wire contraptions we felt sure had been set to trap us. They were, we learnt later, actually Heligoland traps for catching not boys but birds. Understandably we didn't think of this at the time as we certainly hadn't seen any birds except one and that, bizarrely, had been a Great Spotted Woodpecker flying around frantically, presumably searching forlornly for trees scorched to the ground by the holocaust. As the sun sank lower we reached the lighthouse. It was real but deserted.

The path close by led us to a line of little grey cottages mysteriously fortified by a circular moat which encircled them. The moat held not water, but more traps. This was Dungeness Bird Observatory. We knocked nervously. The door creaked open. The only inhabitants were a few more tremulous schoolboys. They reassured us that we had come to the right place. They explained that the lighthouse used to be nearer the sea, but the shingle desert was growing almost by the minute so that the English Channel was now a further half mile away, hidden behind a vast bank of pebbles. They would show it to us the next day if the shingle hadn't spread across to France by then. They also showed us the little kitchen where we would have been able to cook supper if we'd remembered to bring any food. We hadn't. So they kindly lent us a slice or two of bread and a spoonful of tea. They then showed us to a dormitory dripping with soggy anoraks and musty wellies, and we gratefully collapsed on small wooden bunks and fell sound asleep.

This is a Heligoland trap and . . .   . . . these are people trying to catch a bird in one

For a fuller explanation see next chapter; meanwhile . . . read on . . .

A couple of hours later we were woken up. It may have been more than a couple of hours but it was certainly still dark. A loud and fearsome voice was booming: 'Come on, come on, let's get round the traps.' This, we were told, was the warden. The warder? No, the warden. The warden of Dungeness Bird Observatory in those days was Bert Axell, known today, more reverently, as Herbert Axell or H.E. Axell, undoubtedly one of Britain's most distinguished ornithologists. Be that as it may, to me and the other quivering schoolboys back in 1957 he was a figure of fear and mystery. Throughout the ten days I don't think I ever saw his face. He roused us from our beds well before sunrise and herded us out into the trapping area under cover of darkness. All we saw was a large muffled shape marching ahead of us brandishing a big wooden staff. As we approached a Heligoland trap the shape would drop back behind us and he would chivvy us into position, prodding us gently but forcefully with his stick. If we were slow, he prodded us quite hard. In this way, each morning, we would catch White-throats. We couldn't *see* them, but they were there all right, cowering in the bushes after a hard night's migration, hoping to slip out of England across the Channel on their way south as soon as the sun rose. Very few escaped. They were hemmed in by dozy schoolboys, chivvied down into the funnel of the traps and into the catching boxes. Then the warden, with amazing sleight of hand would whip them out of the boxes and into little bags, like a conjurer palming white rabbits. For all we saw of them they could have *been* white rabbits! At breakneck speed we'd be hustled round about a dozen or more traps, and, at each one, a bag would be filled up with more Whitethroats. The round completed, the warden would accelerate ahead of us, silhouetted against the dawn sky, his stick now festooned with clusters of bird bags. Before the rising sun could reveal his features, the door of the ringing room would slam in our faces. *Our* work was ended, as the warden's presumably began.

We'd usually go back to bed, or sometimes we'd lurk outside the ringing room hoping to catch a glimpse of Mr Axell. All we ever saw was a hand which popped out of a small window every now and then and released another Whitethroat. I suppose he must have finally emerged about eight o'clock. By this time my eyes were too bleary with fatigue to see what he really looked like. One thing I *did* know about him – he certainly knew how to catch Whitethroats, or rather he certainly knew how to organise schoolboys to catch Whitethroats. We never seemed to catch anything *but* Whitethroats. Not that we ever saw any of them. There must have been thousands in the bushes before first light, as there were certainly hundreds recorded in the observatory's ringing log each day. Yet, if we ever staggered around the area after breakfast, about mid-day usually, there was hardly ever a Whitethroat to be seen. They were presumably somewhere over Paris by then, wearing Dungeness rings.

The routine went on day after day. Me and my chums became increasingly upset. Not that we'd gone down to Dungeness hoping to see Whitethroats; but not only did we not see many Whitethroats – we didn't see many other birds either. We *had* rather hoped that the point of going to a bird observatory was to observe birds. Instead we were being herded through gorse bushes in pitch darkness, prodded with a big stick and being shown virtually nothing. Frankly, after a week of this, we were a little bruised and a lot exhausted. The moat and the barbed wire encircling Dungeness seemed ominously appropriate. We joked that the observatory felt more like a prison camp, yet the joke seemed rather flat when one day one of my companions, a strapping lad of sixteen, literally broke down in tears. We planned to escape. Late morning of 5 September we packed sandwiches and made a dash for it. We ran the several miles over the shingle desert to the town of Lydd, hitched a ride on a passing army truck and headed for the border.

Wicks and Midrips may sound like a firm of solicitors but it was in fact the name of some nice little pools on the boundary of Kent and Sussex. They've dried up now but in the fifties they were the home of something we hadn't seen much of at Dungeness – birds. My single page of notes from the so-called holiday refers to that day.

'September 5th: Wicks and Midrips.'

The writing is understandably squiggly and nervous; it is clearly that of a disturbed teenage boy suffering from physical exhaustion and mental stress. There's a nice, if wobbly, list of Waders (including a Red-necked Phalarope) but clearly my powers of observation had been severely affected. It is some indication of how deranged I had become that the entry in my notebook consists mainly of puzzled jottings and distorted sketches of two mystery birds. On happier days I'd have known perfectly well what they were, but by the end of the week, I'd been reduced to such a state that I couldn't even recognise Ruffs!

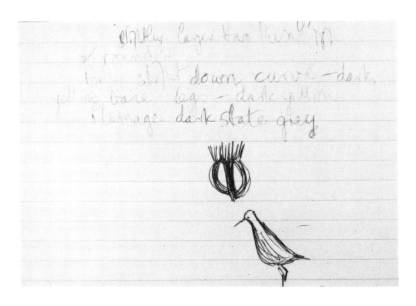

Dungeness –
the mirage.

The reality

If you'd like to visit Dunge now,
write to:
    Sean McMinn (Warden)
    Dungeness Bird Observatory
    Romney Marsh
    Kent

The observatory –
the house on the
end with the
birders' cars
outside it.

It's quite possible that I and my pals were nasty bolshy little schoolboys who thoroughly deserved to be thrashed through the gorse bushes in the dead of night, and I dare say Mr Axell's rumbustious manner with a big knobbly stick concealed a heart of gold. Or maybe he had an ulcer that week; or had just dipped out on a lifer. It's also possible that *he* hated getting up to catch Whitethroats just as much as we did, but that it was an unavoidable part of the job which he was forced to do by some greater authority. Maybe it was in the contract for the Dungeness warden in those days: 'Ring 500 Whitethroats a day, or you're out on your ear.' If this *was* the case, no wonder he seemed a bit sulky, and no wonder he took it out on us. I *do* know that from that day to this H.E. Axell has chalked up a most impressive list of ornithological achievements, most notably, guiding the development and management of the superb RSPB reserve at Minsmere during the sixties and seventies (cf. Axell, H. and Hosking, E., *Minsmere: Portrait of a Bird Reserve*). Mind you, I do seem to recall Minsmere at that time being almost as difficult to get *into* as Dungeness was to get *out* of, so perhaps we did rather favour the firm hand, but then that's often necessary to protect birds from human interference, including bird-watchers.

Anyway, I hope it will be taken only in a spirit of relative frivolity if I say that that week at Dungeness nearly put me off bird-watching for life! One of my friends, the one who wept, *did* vow he'd never visit a bird observatory again and went back to train-spotting. *I* went back to Bartley reservoir, and soon after that to an observatory where the previous year I, and many other young bird-watchers, had received a thoroughly delightful welcome. This was Monk's House Bird Observatory in Northumberland.

My first visit there had been so enjoyable that perhaps Dunge simply couldn't follow it. The event took place just pre-notebook and so is undocumented, but I suspect it must

have been late March or early April 1956 – presumably during
the Easter holidays, in a year when Easter fell early. I remember it was fairly cold and there were still wintry birds about. I
was fifteen, it was my first bird holiday and I went with
another boy from school who was, if anything, an even less
experienced birder than me. I know it was a long journey.
We went on a big train from Birmingham to Newcastle and
then transferred to a smaller train: no doubt steam in those
days, to make it even more romantic. I remember getting my
first tick of the trip from the train window – a single
Whooper Swan on a gravel pit somewhere near Durham. I
remember being quite sure it wasn't a Bewick's, and the fact
that it was a single bird so far north would suggest I was right.
Actually, if I close my eyes, I can see it clearly, and there *is* an
awful lot of yellow on the beak.

The local train took us somewhere else but I can't
remember where. Then I think we caught a bus and I have a
vague recall at getting off at the Northumbrian fishing
village of Seahouses. We may well have got off one stop too
early, as we then had to walk up the coast road towards
Bamburgh. It must have been late afternoon as we passed a
rather fetching little marshy pool by the roadside which held
a few Pintails and various Waders. I didn't know it then, but
it looked very like the main flood at Upton Warren – very
nice. It was nearly evening when we arrived at Monk's
House Bird Observatory. The building was situated literally
on the seashore about half way between Seahouses and
Bamburgh. Come to think of it now, it was a very untypical
location for a bird observatory. Most of them are perched out
on promontories or stuck on islands, in places with special
geographical reasons for catching the displaced flow of
migrating birds. Monk's House was simply a spot somewhere along a more or less dead straight line of coast – it
didn't even stick out a bit. This no doubt explains why it very
rarely recorded any rare birds. This wasn't something that

ever much bothered me or any of the other visitors. Monk's House had much more to offer than *just* rare birds. For a start, the building itself was truly delightful, a sort of glorified cottage or small country mansion built in soft grey stone and covered with ivy. It looked as if it had been transplanted from the Cotswolds. It was actually more properly titled Monk's House Bird Observatory and Field Centre, and people came to study not only birds but also plants and rocks, and particularly seaweed, shrimps, molluscs and other wiggly things generally found in rock pools. In fact most of the young people staying there were university students doing a marine biology course. They enjoyed superb facilities. They could relax in comfy chairs in a spacious sitting-room with a sea view; they could study in an excellent library or a small well-equipped laboratory; they ate delicious food in a delightful dining-room that looked like a Cornish tea shoppe, with vases of flowers and fascinating wildlife pictures all over the walls; and they slept in cosy dormitories. *We* were put in a grotty little caravan outside. This was fair enough; we *were* grotty little schoolboys and we'd probably booked rather late. Actually, it was rather good. The caravan was round the back, right on the sea-shore, and was anchored to the observatory to prevent it floating away on a high tide. We felt like Arctic explorers as, all through the night, the waves literally sprayed the windows and we were buffeted by a howling wind. But it wasn't the gale that kept us awake – it was excitement.

We were willingly up at dawn and tottered out to our first experience of a Northumbrian shoreline. Up until then my list was missing any number of relatively common seabirds. After a few minutes the sun had risen to illuminate several 'ticks'. There were black and white Eider Drakes bobbing on the water, calling to their ducks with that wonderful 'ooo . . . oo . . . ooo' that sounds like a cross between a shocked old lady and Frankie Howerd. There were Fulmars, skimming around like small gliders. In the mid-fifties they were only just beginning to work their way down Britain from Scotland and the breeding colony on Bamburgh Castle was one of the furthest south. On the rocks, huddled amongst the seaweed, a new Wader – Purple Sandpipers. It was a magical start to my first bird holiday: majestic scenery, new birds and a good breakfast. That first visit lasted about a week and my notebooks record three further visits: a repeat run the following April and autumn visits in August of 1957 and 1958. My memories of Monk's House are very happy. For that, I would without doubt, have to thank the warden, the late Dr E.A.R. Ennion, and his wife, Dorothy.

In *The Living Birds of Eric Ennion* (Gollancz) he tells us that as a schoolboy birder and artist he was himself something of a loner: 'Nor do I ever remember having any help from anyone in sketching nor until very much later in watching birds.' Perhaps nevertheless he felt the lack of adult guidance and had resolved to give the youngsters what he himself lacked. Personally I am very aware of a great debt of gratitude to two adults who gave enormous encouragement to me and to so many other young bird-watchers throughout their lifetimes. They were both superb birders, magnificent artists and delightful people. One was R.A. (Richard) Richardson at Cley and the other Dr Ennion at Monk's House. These two men were truly teachers, and they taught not only how to watch birds but how to enjoy them. I think too they both liked *people* and consequently people liked them. Especially young people, to whom they passed on their knowledge with infinite generosity, patience and good humour. We always knew Eric Ennion as 'Doctor' – 'Doctor Ennion'. It seemed appropriate, as his very presence was comforting. He looked relaxed and jovial; portly, but very fit and healthy; round face, smiling and rather bald, with tufts of curly white hair. A veritable Mr Pickwick of the bird world. He had that special teacher's gift of instantly remembering every youngster's name and making them feel as if they were getting special attention. Our days were organised but never regimented — exactly what inexperienced birders needed. Each day we would tumble into the back of his rather dilapidated van and Dr Ennion would give us a guided tour of the many and varied delights of Northumbrian birding. The wonder of Northumberland is that there are so many very different types of habitat within one county, many of them within a short van drive of Monk's House. We drove inland to the Cheviot Hills, where we flushed Red Grouse from the heather and Woodcock from the birch woods, and watched Dippers on the rocky streams. We scanned the mud flats at Budle Bay for Waders and the bushes on Holy Island for small migrants. We sailed out to the Farne Islands to study the teeming colonies of Auks and Terns, and we sat for hours on the Stagg Rocks at Bamburgh learning the taxing art of sea-watching. It was never boring, quite simply because Dr Ennion showed us exactly what birds to look for, how to identify them and, best of all, how to draw them. Before our very eyes he'd dash off on-the-spot sketches in his extraordinary energetic style made up of straight lines and jagged angles. Ennion's work is instantly recognisable. It is not detailed, it is often 'impressionistic' and it sometimes almost borders on caricature, yet few bird artists can capture the jizz, movement and atmosphere of birds the way he did. If only I'd kept my notebooks from that time — full of genuine Ennion originals!

I saw plenty of new birds on my visits. Most of them were local specialities: Velvet Scoter and Red-necked Grebes on the sea watches; Roseate Terns on the Farnes; the Dippers and the Grouse and so on. I didn't ever see anything really unusual at Monk's House, though certainly by my third and fourth visits I was becoming more rarity conscious. I always visited Holy Island with some sense of nervous anticipation, especially if I'd just been browsing through old copies of the

Northumberland Bird Report. Holy Island has had some pretty good birds but *I* was never really lucky. Blue-headed Wagtails and migrant Warblers were nice but hardly 'cripplers'. As my anxiety to see rare birds increased, so my imagination developed and my accuracy diminished.

One August morning I spotted a couple of distant Storm Petrels through the observatory's telescope, which was permanently set up at the sitting-room window trained on the sea – a terrible temptation to string if you got it to yourself! I succumbed later in the day by claiming an adult Long-tailed Skua about a mile out. Closing my eyes now and re-viewing that bird, I seriously think it was in fact a second-year Gannet! . . . *two* miles out? I also worked very hard one evening in Seahouses harbour with an 'Iceland Gull' with 'biscuit coloured' primaries and a black bill – in mid-August! No doubt a moulty old Herring Gull.

During my second autumn visit I became almost obsessed with the fact that I'd never seen a Red-backed Shrike. Some of my more playful companions must have noticed, as, one evening, they sent me off to Budle Bay saying that a 'probable Red-backed Shrike' had been seen there earlier in the day. They told me just as the bell was about to ring for supper. They chose their bird well. If it had been a *real* rarity everyone would have leapt into a car there and then and steamed off to Budle Bay. But of course *they'd* all seen Red-backed Shrike, so I wasn't surprised or suspicious when no-one else wanted to go and look for it; but, to a tick-hungry lad of fifteen, a Red-backed Shrike was more filling than roast chicken, so off I went. I half ran and half hitch-hiked several miles up the coast, trudged round Budle Bay for a couple of hours, scanning all the hawthorn bushes and telegraph posts – they'd even told me which was its favourite post (right over the far side, of course!) – and, as darkness fell, I limped back home to find an inexplicably chucklesome gathering waiting for me, enjoying their bedtime cocoa. I suppose they were hoping I'd claim to have seen the Shrike (which, of course, didn't exist) but I think I knew I'd better not. Instead I gamely insisted that Curlews at sunset were better than a rotten old Shrike any day and hobbled off to bed, hoping I still had a Mars bar hidden under my pillow. I must have been a naive young lad and forgiving too! Nowadays I'd be much more ruthless. I'd pay them back with a 'possible immature Bonaparte's Gull that flew in with the Black-headeds to roost'. They'd have been stuck out at Budle Bay every supper time for the rest of the week!

Monk's House – photographic memories through a 'Brownie'!
1. The house on the shore.
2. The caravan on the shore.
3. The shore.
4. The distant Farnes from Seahouses.
5. Landing on Inner Farne.

A miscellany of out-of-focus, badly framed Farne bird life.

The fact is, though, I don't really remember Monk's House for the birds I saw so much as the birds I *caught* – or helped to catch – for it was there that I was introduced to a whole new aspect of ornithology . . .

7
Trapping and ringing

. . . and not just Whitethroats! The range of species involved in trapping activities at Monk's House was almost
bewildering. The work was organised not only by Dr
Ennion himself but by various pioneers of British ringing
who were Monk's House regulars. They demonstrated many
ingenious and bizarre methods of attempting to catch birds
and also instructed us in the skills of handling and ringing the
ones that didn't get away. We schoolboys were not merely
used, we were *involved*.

There were two permanent traps at Monk's House. The
most obvious being, as at most bird observatories, the
Heligoland in the 'Obs' garden. A Heligoland trap, by the
way (in case you don't know; forgive me if you do) is a large
funnel-shaped construction made of chicken-wire stretched
over big wooden poles, usually about six feet high. A small
team of ringers and their helpers (schoolboys will do very
well) drive or chivvy the birds into the mouth of the funnel
and up into the narrow end. They (the ringers) try to guide
the birds in by making rather odd 'shushing' or 'pishing'
noises. It's strange that a 'pishing' noise is sometimes also used
by bird-watchers in woods to lure birds closer. In this case,
it's meant to drive them away! Or at least ahead. It usually
works, which may explain why 'pishing' in woods often
doesn't! Actually it all depends how you pish. If you pish
successfully when driving a heligoland the bird will scuttle
ahead of you up the funnel and into an end compartment that

can be sealed off by the head trapper (or ringer) shutting the door. He does this by pulling a carefully rigged piece of string, which is usually knotted loosely over a rusty nail stuck in one of the poles at the mouth of the trap. Whilst he's struggling to untie the knot, his helpers will attempt to dissuade the bird from flying back over his shoulder by more pishing and by clapping their hands. This is often mistaken for sarcastic applause that the head ringer has at last managed to untie the knot and pull the door shut. Or it maybe genuine admiration that he's managed actually to catch a bird. In point of fact, he still hasn't *quite* caught it yet. The bird is now in the end compartment and feeling understandably claustrophobic. It sees what appears to be its only escape route. At the very narrowest end of the funnel is a small wooden box. This is clearly where the bird is meant to end up. However, it appears as if the berk who built the box ran out of wood and has left the end wall off. The bird makes a gleeful leap for freedom, only to bonk its beak on a glass window – the end wall of the box. This certainly doesn't hurt the bird but it tends to discourage it and, realising it has been fairly nabbed, it will sit and wait to be taken out of the catching box, which has meanwhile been totally sealed off by the ringer releasing another little door, by pulling another piece of string, to another round of applause. The bird is then removed from the box by the ringer, who sticks his hand in through a sleeve pinned over a hole in the side of the box. Often the sleeve really *is* a sleeve, taken from a smelly old jacket, or sometimes it is a piece of smelly old sock with the foot cut off, or it may be a short section of trouser leg (a pair of discarded corduroys can be dissected into at least four excellent catching box sleeves). If the berk who made the box has made it too big, the bird will be able to flatten itself up in one corner, and the ringer will just not *quite* be able to reach it! Birds seem to suss this game very quickly and thoroughly enjoy flitting playfully from corner to corner just out of reach of grasping

fingertips. The ringer pulls several muscles contorting his
arm, till eventually the bird gets bored and, longing to see the
open air again, allows itself to be gently removed, popped in
a bag and taken back to the observatory. There, it is weighed,
measured, ringed and released and, with any luck, it will also
be identified – though I have known ringers so absorbed in
their statistics that they have omitted to note what species
they have caught! I daresay a few rarities have been thrown
away like this. Heligoland traps are usually built over part of
the observatory garden. Frankly, the Heligoland at Monk's
House wasn't much of a trap, mainly because there wasn't
much of a garden. I seem to recall a small concrete pond
(complete with gnome perhaps), a row of lettuces and a line
of runner beans on sticks, all of which were meant to lure
small migrants with a drink, fresh greens and a handy perch.
The only bird I remember being caught there was a Willow
Warbler – just one! Nearby, in the dunes, was the second
permanent trap: the inappropriately named 'Crow trap'. A
Crow trap is like a big wire box, about six feet square, with a
small funnel-shaped entrance in the top narrowing downwards. It is usually baited with bits of soggy potato peelings,
old bacon rind and other supposedly irresistible left-overs,
like cold porridge and tea bags. Crows are supposed to drop
down the funnel in order to get at the bait and be so daft that
they can't find their way out again. Crows are in fact
renowned for not being at all daft and they don't usually
bother to go in in the first place. In fact, the one bird I've *never*
known to get caught in a Crow trap is a Crow. Starlings, on
the other hand, are foolish enough not only to enjoy eating
cold porridge and tea bags but also to get themselves caught
in the process. Instead of calmly working out that they can fly
up and out the way they flew down and in (as the wise Crow
no doubt would) Starlings panic. They flap around squawk-
ing and squealing until the ringer comes and takes them out.
If Crow traps were renamed Starling traps they could be

considered pretty successful . . . as was the one at Monk's
House.

**Heligoland
traps**

Heligoland trap over bushes.

Birders 'chivvying' and 'pishing'.

The catching box – cheap version, using perspex
instead of glass. The sleeve is on the other side.

Crow trap

Bird goes in here

and is chivvied
into here

. . . or not.

However, the main disadvantage with both Heligoland and Crow traps is that they don't move. The birds have to be lured or persuaded to go *into* the trap. In the mid-fifties the great breakthrough occurred – traps that could be taken *to* the birds.

It was about this time that the first mist nets were imported into England from Japan. The Japanese had apparently been using them successfully for donkey's years, but in Japan the birds that were caught ended up in sweet and sour sauce. The pioneer ringers of Monk's House were some of the first to use mist nets for more constructive and instructive purposes. I well remember being shown, along with other wide-eyed youngsters, my first mist net. We gathered round Dr Ennion like children round Father Christmas as he carefully unwrapped the neat parcel and revealed what looked like a large tangled hair net. We were told that ringers had to undergo months of rigorous training with Mist nets – and that was just to learn how to unravel them! Then you had to learn how to put them up. A mist net *is* like a big hair-net. It is a large rectangle of very fine mesh which is threaded on *four* slightly thicker strands forming *three* panels. Honestly it does, look at the drawing. Each of the thicker strands has a loop at the end

– so that's *four* loops each side, right? These loops have to be threaded over a bamboo pole. There are *two* poles. If you do it right, the rectangle will therefore be stretched between the poles. If you do it wrong . . . it looks like a huge cat's cradle. The first trick is to ensure that you thread the loops in the right order on the right (or left!) pole. Months of research by ham-fingered ringers led to the invention of little bits of coloured string, which could be tied round the loops to identify them. Soon after that, some genius came up with small pieces of cardboard with four slots in them, on which the loops could be fastened neatly for storage. Once the net is threaded on the poles, the poles have to be securely stuck in the ground. So the next development in the art was the introduction of a carrier bag full of tent pegs and longer bits of string to be used as guy ropes. If you'd forgotten your tent pegs, you could tie the guys around stones. Once the mist net is up it is, as it were, a freestanding wall of very fine mesh. The birds can't see it. The problem is, neither can the ringer. The first thing a new mist-netter usually catches is himself. You can easily hear a team of mist-netters at work: the woods echo with cries of 'Look out', 'Mind the net' and 'Oh ★★★! I'm caught again.' Naturally such a row tends to scare the birds away. Not that you'd be able to do any incidental bird-watching, as you have to take your binoculars off whilst putting up the nets, otherwise they'd dangle down and get hopelessly entangled. However, the great thing about mist nets is that once you *have* got them up, and disengaged yourself, you *can* go away and do a bit of birding, or set up another lot of nets. You simply leave the nets for a short while and let the birds catch themselves. Occasionally, a bit of chivvying or 'pishing' is done by a team of ringers strolling in a line through the woods, like policemen on a crime hunt. But if you've put up the net in the right place, this shouldn't be necessary. Mist nets really *do* work when cannily situated.

There were several nice little woods near Monk's House

that had had little gullies cleared through them especially for the nets. This also kept them out of the wind: important, since once a net is ruffled by the wind it tends to billow and becomes visible. Also, in rain, drops of water cling to it, so it looks like a giant dew-covered spider's web, and again the birds will avoid it, since they presumably have no wish to be consumed by a giant spider. On a calm day the net is invisible. A flock of small birds working their way blithely through the woods will come across an apparently empty gully, innocently flit across it and be arrested in mid-air by a mysterious unseen force. It must come as a bit of a surprise, but most birds are philosophical enough to accept it without a struggle. The weight of the bird usually carries it into a little pocket of net which hangs over one of the stronger threads and the bird lies there peacefully swinging as if in a small hammock. I suspect they spend the first few minutes contemplating: 'What the hell happened there?!' They may then jiggle around and try to get out but soon discover that the more they jiggle, the more they get entangled, so they usually give up and wait for the ringer to take them out. This is another skill that requires weeks of training. The secret of getting birds out of mist nets is feet first (the bird's feet, that is). If you free the feet, firmly grip them together with forefinger and thumb of one hand and pull gently, it's amazing how often the rest of the bird will follow. It's then you realise (and maybe so does the bird) that it isn't really tangled in the net at all. You can then deftly slip the other hand over the bird, grip it in the approved manner and take it away for the ringing treatment and release. It's best to take it some way away, as it's no tribute to avian intelligence that many birds, having been thoughtfully released upwards and away, will turn round and fly straight back into the net. Of course sometimes birds *do* get themselves ever so tangled up. Long-tailed Tits are awfully good at it, and we tended to catch a lot at Monk's House. Long-tailed Tits rarely travel

alone, and once one little Tit has dived into a mist net, the rest
of its chums are likely to follow. A net full of Long-tailed Tits
can keep you busy for hours. During my early training I
acquired something of a reputation as an ace Long-tailed Tit
extractor. My nimble little fingers saved many a precious
mist net that might have otherwise to be snipped to ribbons
in order to release a particularly ravelled up bird.

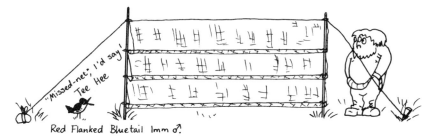

Red Flanked Bluetail Imm ♂.

A mist net This one has been drawn on a windy day so that the net is billowing
and visible, otherwise you wouldn't be able to see it. Unfortunately, this means
the *birds* can see it too and therefore they are wisely refusing to fly into it. This
explains the doleful look on the face of the ringer, who has been put by the net to
give you some idea of scale. This is in fact a very small mist net, otherwise it
wouldn't fit on the page.

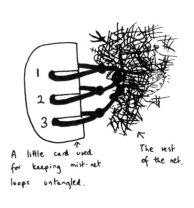

A little card used
for keeping mist-net
loops untangled.

The rest
of the net.

Long-tailed Tit enjoying a kip
in a mist-net "Hammock"...

I know there are many bird lovers who are opposed to trapping birds, even for scientific purposes: people who feel that it is undignified or even possibly harmful. All I would say is that, in many many years of ringing activity, I have never once known of a bird being harmed by the process. Ringers are skilled and careful people, meticulously trained in the handling of even the tiniest and frailest of species. The comfort and safety of the bird always comes first. The work of ringers has without doubt advanced the science of ornithology vastly over recent years, teaching us an enormous amount about migration routes, longevity, moults, ageing, identification and avian biology in general. I'm happy to declare myself one hundred per cent pro-ringing and trapping, and I honestly think those opposed to it are taking a somewhat sentimental standpoint that may even, in the long run, be detrimental to the welfare of the birds themselves. I believe the more we *know*, the more we are likely to *care*.

I would not, mind you, argue that birds actually *enjoy* being caught. It must be a bit humiliating to get stuck in a smelly old Crow trap, and a trifle narking to fly into an invisible wall, but any humiliation or discomfort that birds may experience is definitely far outweighed by the humiliation and discomfort ringers have to go through. At Monk's House I never considered any of the activities to be in any way cruel to the birds, but they were *certainly* cruel to ringers! Indeed the birds were given plenty of opportunity of getting their own back, particularly sea birds and waders. Nowadays mist nets – huge long lines of them – are often used to catch waders, but back in the fifties nobody had thought of that. Besides which we only had a couple of twenty-foot nets, which looked a bit pathetic stuck out on miles of mud. We used to put down wader-traps, which were odd little cages with weird entrances that were *meant* to work on the same principle as Crow traps, i.e. the birds were supposed to be dumb enough to catch themselves. The hope was that, as waders tend to have their eyes down and their beaks in the mud, they wouldn't look where they were going and would walk into one of these little traps. It wasn't likely and it didn't often happen.

More commonly, we used to go clap-netting. This was a real production number. The net itself is rectangular, about four foot by three perhaps, and made of strong cord. It looks like something that might be used by Norwegian fishermen. It is not at all delicate like the Japanese mist net. It is laid out flat on the mud or sand, stretched between two rigid sticks. The sticks are pivotted in the sand by being attached to two large, round eyes (as in 'hook and eye') so that they can swivel on them if yanked by a rope which is attached to the other end of the stick. I'll be honest, I can't really explain how it works, and I find my own description totally confusing! I dare say the whole rig functions on sound geometric principles, but it looks as if it would do credit to Heath Robinson. Anyway, please take my word for it, if you pull on the rope the net will flick over and catch anything that is feeding next to it. Well, that's the theory. There are several flaws and problems. First of all, the net is awfully visible, so it has to be disguised with bits of seaweed, pebbles, dead crabs and so on, so that it looks like a natural part of the beach. Then the ringer has to retire to some distant cover, as it is not likely that any wader is going to wander across to the trap with him standing next to it, holding a highly suspicious piece of rope. We, at Monk's House, were usually trapping on an estuary, so I would hide in the sand dunes, holding the end of about twenty yards of pulling rope. The next problem was how to persuade a Dunlin or Ringed Plover to come and feed within a couple of feet of your diguised net, when it had a couple of hundred yards of shoreline to choose from. You can't lay bait for waders: they don't go much for cold porridge and tea bags. All you can do is wait. So, that's the scene. There I am crouching in the dunes, nervously clutching my twenty yards of rope, which is attached to my clap net out on the mud, camouflaged with pebbles and seaweed. It's mid March on the north-east coast and it's raining. I scared all the birds away when I was putting out the net, so it's bound to be a long wait before they come back. The first possible disaster – I may well huddle up under my Pack-a-mac and fall asleep and, when I wake up, the tide's come in and covered my net. Or maybe I'll just wait and wait, watching the waders scuttling on every yard of beach except where my trap is. I spent many days out there, never once pulling my rope. The only diversions I recall were a pair of Avocets flying over, and a young lady who regularly each afternoon furtively crept into the dunes on the opposite side of the estuary and crouched down for a clandestine wee! Either that, or she was a very shy flasher. Maybe it was Marion from Oak Tree Crescent! Just now and again though, I'd be vigilant and alert and undistracted and a Ringed Plover would actually approach the danger zone. You had to note very carefully that the bird had hit the right spot, which wasn't easy from twenty or thirty yards away. If you waited too long, the bird would trot on by or even fly off. So you had to be decisive, make up your mind and *pull*. Several things could happen . . . or not happen. Sometimes the eye would yank straight out of the sand, the net stay where it was and the bird carry on feeding as if nothing had happened – which it hadn't! Or if you'd gone a bit over the top with the camouflage, the pile of disguising seaweed and pebbles would be so heavy that you'd need a tug of war team to pull the rope. In this case, it would flip over so slowly that the bird would have time to look up, laugh at it and stroll away casually before the net flopped soggily down. Or . . . an over-enthusiastic pull could propel the shower of seaweed and pebbles like shot from a twelve-bore, endangering me and the girl in the dunes and scattering the waders all over the

horizon. If any of these disasters occurred, you had to traipse
out on to the beach and reset the whole thing; thus again
scaring all the birds away for another half hour or so. Just
now and then, though, you got it right. A bold decision, a
deft flick of the wrist and the net would snap over and a
Ringed Plover would be caught. Then you had to race over
before the bird wriggled out from underneath it, like a
commando on an assault course, *and* you had to make sure
you didn't trip over the rope and whip the net away just as
you were about to grab your prize. It *was* a prize. Waders are
to me one of the most fascinating and attractive groups of
birds in the field. In the hand, they are superb value. When
you handle a wader you can't help but be aware that you are
holding a creature not only very specialised and beautiful but
also truly wild. You can't help but be gentle and careful with
them. Frankly, it feels like a privilege and I don't think any
bird-lover could fail to be a little in awe. It was always worth
the wait.

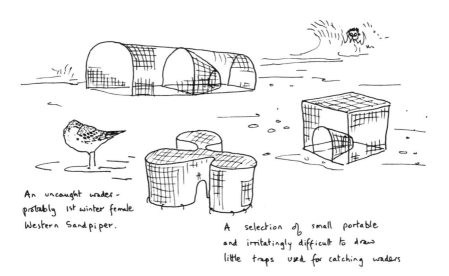

An uncaught wader -
probably 1st winter female
Western Sandpiper.

A selection of small portable
and irritatingly difficult to draw
little traps used for catching waders

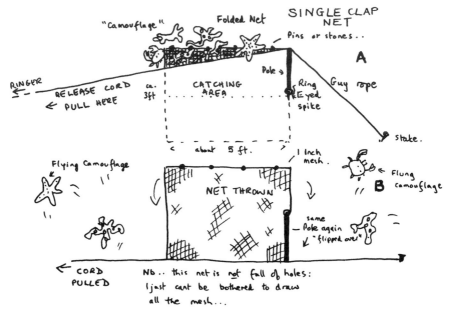

"Camouflage"   Folded Net   SINGLE CLAP NET

Pins or stones..

A

RINGER
←
RELEASE CORD   ca.   CATCHING   Pole →   Ring   Guy rope
← PULL HERE   3ft   .... AREA .....   REyed   spike   Stake.

about 5 ft.   1 inch mesh.

Flying Camouflage

NET THROWN   B   Flung camouflage

same
— Pole again
↙ "flipped over"

← CORD PULLED   NB.. this net is not full of holes: I just cant be bothered to draw all the mesh...

THIS is a diagram of how a CLAP NET works, taken basically from an old book of "How to Trap birds" .... any wiser?

Wader-trapping was not for the faint-hearted. You could catch pneumonia, freeze to death, chafe your hands on the rope or snap your fingers off setting the nets. But at least the birds themselves, once in the hand, were gentleness itself: soft and calm and totally harmless. Not so the sea birds. Every week a boatload of ringers would set off to the Farne Islands to ring young Gulls, Shags and Puffins – a masochist's day-trip, if ever there was one. Young Gulls are every bit as belligerent as their parents and twice as ugly. Strangely enough, they even seem twice as *big*, an illusion created by their puffed-out juvenile plumage. It takes courage even to lay a hand on one – or rather two hands, which is what it takes to control the flailing stubby wings, waggling feet and snapping beaks. Ringing young Gulls requires skill, strength and considerable co-ordination.

Ringing young Shags requires a clothes peg or blocked sinuses. The stench round a Shag's nest is worse than that under a schoolboy's bed. Soggy socks and unwashed underpants have nothing on rotting seaweed mixed with droppings and disgorged fish – which, Lord help them, the baby Shags are supposed to eat! St Francis of Assisi would be pushed to claim that young Shags are endearing. They emerge from the eggs looking like misshapen frogs and mature into something rather less lovely than a pterodactyl. They do indeed gorge themselves on regurgitated fish, though they rarely wait for the adults even to cough it up, choosing to stab their ferocious little beaks ungraciously straight down Mummy's throat. This creates the bizarre illusion that the parent is trying to swallow her offspring. I'm not sure which is the least appetising thought – eating a young Shag, or a pile of pre-chewed mackerel! Of course adult Shags are *not* cannibals, and indeed they are very attractive birds, especially in their sleek breeding dress of glossy green scales, buttercup face masks, and rather fetching little quiffs. It's some consolation to a ringer to remind himself that these unlovely babies will grow up to look so nice, as he tries to close the ring without throwing up all over the nest. True to form, the young Shag usually throws up all over him. It's a defence mechanism, similar to the Fulmar spitting out foul-smelling oil. It works. Like I said, the birds have a way of getting their own back! None more effectively than the supposedly cute little Puffins.

Puffins may well look like portly little old gentlemen in dinner suits but they are elderly delinquents when they are roused. Mind you, I don't blame them. In order to ring them we did indeed rouse them. The whole business had to be very carefully timed so as not to disturb the bird's breeding cycle. Puffins on the Farnes (as in many of their colonies) nest in old rabbit warrens. For a week or so before they lay their eggs they go house-hunting and in late March they check out the holes before deciding on a cosy one. The Farnes are riddled with these burrows and, as you walk across an apparently deserted old warren, you are probably literally treading on several Puffins. You can't see them, but they're down there, considering how they're going to decorate their new home, cuddling their mates or having a nap. If you want to ring them, you have to tread carefully so as not to collapse the burrows, kneel down by the entrance and stick your hand down the hole. If you feel nothing – it's almost a relief. If there's a Puffin in there, you'll soon know. You'll be lucky to get your hand back. Those pretty little rainbow beaks can snip your fingers off like a pair of garden secateurs. I used to wear a large pair of motor-cyclist's gauntlets. I'd hold the Puffin's body firmly in one hand and its beak in the other. Puffins are intelligent birds and they quickly realised they were being inconvenienced in the interests of science. They soon calmed down and I was able to release the beak. They'd simply stare quizzically at me as I shook off one glove to reach for the rings. Then they'd lacerate my bare hand with their feet!! Those sweet orange tootsies have claws on them like buckthorns, and they are all the more effective because you expect the attack to come from the other end. After a couple of hours ringing Puffins I looked as if I'd been molested by a werewolf. Comical old gentlemen indeed! The Puffins came to no harm. Having acquired their shining new rings – which looked rather smart against their orange ankles – they were popped back into their burrows and they carried on with the business of mating and egg-laying.

There was also much ringing activity carried on at night. So weird and embarassing were some of these antics that it's no wonder many of them took place under cover of darkness. If anyone had *seen* us, we'd have been a laughing stock or arrested for suspicious behaviour. We often used to go dazzling. This method of bird-catching is based on the 'rabbit in the headlamps' principle. You may well have noted that bunnies scampering across the road at night have a dreadful suicidal compulsion to stop, sit down and stare straight at the on-coming beam rather than scoot out of the way. The fact is, a bright enough light sort of hypnotises most creatures to the extent that you can often pick them up. It doesn't harm them to be dazzled – except of course the thousands of rabbits sadly squashed on roads every year. It allows ringers to ring birds almost literally in their sleep (the bird's sleep, that is). We ringers didn't *get* much sleep, as we sloshed across mud flats in the dead of night hoping to trip over roosting Redshanks, or scrambled around derelict farmhouses flashing our torches on snoozing Swallows. This could actually be a very pretty sight, as in the autumn the spotlight would often fall on a beamful of fully grown young Swallows huddled up together shoulder to shoulder, like a

bunch of Bluebirds in a Disney cartoon. One of us would hold the light on them whilst another ringer would creep up behind, gently remove the birds and quickly slip the ring on their feet. Sometimes they'd hardly open their eyes throughout the whole process. They could be popped back on their beams and they'd nod off again as the light was dimmed and we tip-toed away, usually tripping headlong over a ploughshare on the way out.

The silliest night-time expeditions were when we went bat-fowling. Bat-fowling had nothing to do with bats or fowls. I have no idea where the name came from. As it turned out, it was another mysteriously inappropriate term for catching Starlings. A bat-fowling net is wonderfully absurd. It is made of netted string loosely stretched across an oblong framework on a handle. It looks rather like a lacrosse racket, except that it's twelve feet long! The ringer uses two of them, one handle in each hand, and they are hinged together so that they can be clapped shut. We used to set off after dark to scale the slopes of Bamburgh Castle armed with our bat-fowling nets. Bamburgh Castle was, and still is, an imposing and impregnable fortress surrounded by a moat and forbidding battlements, designed effectively to repel marauding vandals . . . and ringers. The slopes are pretty steep and it wasn't easy staggering up them in slippery wellies on a pitch-black moonless windy wet night. The castle walls were covered in ivy and in the ivy roosted hundreds of Starlings. We chose pitch-black moonless windy wet nights so that the birds wouldn't see us coming in the dark nor hear us above the howl of the gale. Once at the foot of the battlements, the ringer would gingerly raise his pair of giant lacrosse rackets over his head. Then he'd spread them flat against the ivy. Then rattle them. The Starlings would then scatter from their leafy beds like a flock of bats (maybe that's where the name came from). You then clamped the nets together, hoping to trap not only a bunch of ivy but also a bunch of Starlings. The sudden movement and the weight of the catch made the precarious poles even harder to hold upright. At this point the gale would often catch the nets like a wind surfer's sails, and the ringer would be whisked off the top of a slope in a short and spectacularly unsuccessful hand-glide. The golden rule was that, whether you got air-borne or crashed into the moat, you *mustn't let go of the poles.* If you did manage to hold the nets together, you did usually catch a fair number of Starlings and House Sparrows. You probably also broke the net . . . and your leg.

Bat-fowling The ringer is panicking because the wind has caught the net and he is now travelling at 1500 feet. The book on *How to Trap Birds* says: 'The net can be worked single-handed, the operator carrying a torch strapped to his head.' The torch should be red, as a warning to other aircraft.

Still, if you thought *that* was silly . . .

On hot August afternoons we went catching Eiders. Like most Wild-fowl, Eiders in Northumberland moult their flight feathers and for a short period even the adults cannot fly well, if at all. There are also lots of full-grown young around with the same problem. Little packs of flightless Eiders gathered in Budle Bay, a large sea loch that at low tide is reduced to a vast expanse of mud, crisscrossed by a few deep and treacherous channels. The Eiders would often snooze on the mud, and our furtive little team of ringers would attempt to creep up on them and nab them. This rarely worked, as the cries of schoolboys sinking into quicksands usually woke them up. The Northumbrian holidaymakers were then treated to the spectacle of half a dozen human beings chasing a pack of tubby little Ducks across the bay, every now and then diving at them in a frantic rugby tackle. The Ducks had the advantage of webbed feet and invariably escaped. They didn't, however, really have anywhere to escape *to*, except into one of the creeks. So we moved on to the second phase of the operation. We would herd a gaggle of Eiders into the water and chivvy them up into the narrowest part, with a few of us lining the banks clapping and 'pishing' so that they didn't scuttle off over the mud again. Then came the really daft part. A couple of intrepid ringers would take to the water, dive under the surface and attempt to come up close enough to an Eider to grab it! It was a wonderful sight. Eiders are, of course, expert divers so, no sooner did a ringer's head pop up in the middle of the flock, than all the birds would pop *down*. Then the ringer would dive and the ducks would all pop up again. Ringers and Eiders would be bobbing up and down like corks; the humans choking and the birds quacking away merrily, no doubt chuckling their beaks off. I always hoped a ringer would surface with an Eider sitting on his head, but it never happened. We all felt honour bound to have a go. It would have been soppy not to. I was not well suited to the task as I am not awfully relaxed in water. I don't so much dive as sink and on the one occasion I was rash enough to try it, I nearly drowned. All I caught was a cold. I think they ended up ringing *me*.

Despite the absurdity and discomfort of it all, we *did* catch lots of birds at Monk's House, and I wouldn't have missed the experience for the world. Techniques were improved and the cause of ornithological science undoubtedly served and, if the Puffins and Eiders were anything to go by, I suspect even the birds themselves were appreciative and entertained. It must be awfully boring sitting in a rabbit-burrow all day or moulting on the mud, and I dare say they looked forward to a bit of fun with the ringers every now and again.

Catching Eiders This ringer is so absorbed in his work that he is totally unaware that he is in fact wearing Britain's first Spectacled Eider . . .

I carried my new-found enthusiasm back home and soon had my garden at Oak Tree Crescent laid out like a mini observatory. I was, at first, too young to qualify as a proper official ringer, so I purchased a stock of small plastic rings, which were put on to the bird's leg by means of a little aluminium spoon. I don't know where I got them all from; I suspect they were advertised in one of those small ads in the Saturday morning papers, along with ex-army binoculars and thermal underwear. My traps were small home-made drop-traps, little wire cages with hinged doors, propped up with a piece of twig. The twig was yanked away by a length of string, which I pulled from the cover of the kitchen window. I caught House Sparrows, Dunnocks, Blackbirds, Song Thrushes, Starlings, Greenfinches, Chaffinches, and lots and lots of Blue Tits. One of the problems was that I wasn't that much of a handyman with my chickenwire, and most of my traps had a few gaps at the corners so they weren't entirely Blue Tit-proof. I had to be pretty quick once I'd pulled the string and belt down the garden before the tiny tits escaped. Eventually I started using my Granny. I'd get her to hold the string at the kitchen window whilst I hid in the garden shed half way down the lawn. Her eyesight wasn't up to much. She wouldn't really have noticed a Vulture in the trap, let alone a Blue Tit, so I had to signal to her by waving a white hankie when a bird was on the bait. She'd pull the string and I'd leap out and nab the Blue Tit. I documented all my catches at the back of my notebook. I noted the species, sex and age, measurements of bill, tail, tarsus and wing, and the date and the colour of the ring. If Granny was not around to help, I'd have to hold the bird in my right hand and write with my left. If Granny *was* around, I'd use her as secretary and she'd write down the information in her trembling longhand. Either way it was almost illegible!

I kept up my garden colour ringing programme for nearly four years and am not really sure what my statistics taught me. They proved that one of my resident Dunnocks had lasted at least three years, and that most of my Greenfinches were merely passing through; but I think I knew that anyway. What I *did* learn, though, was how to handle birds, measure them and read wing formulas, etc. With the benefit of further qualified instruction at bird observatories, and my coming of appropriate age, I was eventually able to qualify for a full licence. I soon owned my own stock of real BTO

(British Trust for Ornithology) rings, my proper pliers and even my own mist nets. During my late teens I was a pretty avid ringer. My early misdemeanours as an egg collector even came in useful as I was an expert at finding nests. I ringed a lot of young birds, making sure I got the youngsters at exactly the right time. Too young and the ring will drop off; too old, and they'll spill out all over the place before they can properly fly. I found a Greenfinch roost in a hawthorn gully at Bartley Reservoir, and could guarantee a net-full of birds any evening there. I must have ringed hundreds of birds. Alas, I only ever had one recovery: not a very apt word for a Greenfinch killed by a cat, a mile from where I'd caught it.

I remember my ringing days with great nostalgia and affection, and indeed amusement. But maybe I didn't always enjoy it as much as I thought. There's an entry in my 1958 notebook, part of a summary of an August trip to Monk's House, and it reads:

> Trapping experience underlined, sometimes painfully, that all methods have great weaknesses. Clap-netting for waders becomes almost nonsensical when carried on in a large unrestricted area and it is often fruitless to continue in the face of the tide. Mist nets, often brilliantly effective, can be little less than aggravating when used either in front of taller bushes, when birds fly over, or in a breeze of any appreciable force, when birds bounce out. Unless ideal conditions can be attained — a small area and favourable tide for clap nets, and low cover and no wind for mist nets — trapping can obviously test the ornithologist's patience to breaking point, and one bird caught is a rarely satisfying reward for hours of discomfort. Despite the fact that the statement must be directly opposed to the essential ringing spirit, I cannot help but feel that, unless a certain measure of success is assured, trapping can not only be irritating and tedious, but it can also squander time which could be

better employed in the pursuit of more fundamental and more entertaining aspects of ornithology, such as thorough sight-survey of an area, or competent identification. Let us have moderation in all things.

So there! My my, how pompous one can be at seventeen (well *I* obviously was)!

In 1981 Dr Eric Ennion died. Monk's House Bird Observatory had closed down years before. It was commemorated in Ennion's own book, *The House on the Shore*, now alas out of print. If you can get a copy please do so; then pass it on to me. Meanwhile rush out and buy *The Living Birds of Eric Ennion* (Gollancz) and enjoy the words and pictures of a most remarkable man.

Dungeness Bird Observatory is still, however, very much alive. In fact, it's an *excellent* place. It's still not exactly pretty . . . the shingle plains are still as desolate as the Gobi Desert and the lighthouse is even further from the sea. It is also now towered over by a gigantic nuclear power-station. In fact, to be honest, the whole area is incredibly ugly! But it's *still* an excellent place. For a start, the atmosphere at the observatory is one of the most amiable in Britain. Every visitor is exhorted to become 'a friend of Dungeness Observatory' – not an invitation I felt inclined to accept back in the fifties, but I certainly am now. Wardens come and go, but they're all nice. There are less Heligolands these days but lots of mist netting, and if you pop down at weekends you are likely to enjoy an informal guided tour of the trapping area and the birds conducted by Peter Grant – one of the hottest birders in the land and the friendliest of all of Dungeness's many friends. Even the monstrous power-station has benefited the area, releasing an offshore outflow of warm water known as 'the patch' which attracts fish, rare Terns and sea-watchers alike. Nearby there are several superb gravel pits, managed by the R S P B, and as long as you've got a car, a bike or strong legs, there's an awful lot to be seen, all splendidly accessible. I thoroughly recommend it.

I am no longer a qualified ringer. Soon after moving to London in the mid sixties I let my licence lapse, as I simply hadn't got enough time to be a ringer *and* a bird-watcher – the two are not necessarily compatible! Mind you, I'm still an energetic chivvier and my fingers, though ageing yearly, are still pretty deft when it comes to extracting entangled Long-tailed Tits. When I visit bird observatories I'm usually allowed to help. For introducing me to this greater involvement, my thanks must go to Monk's House; but for introducing me to birds, birders and the whole nitty-gritty of birding it's definitely thanks to . . . (answer on p. 154 after the pictures).

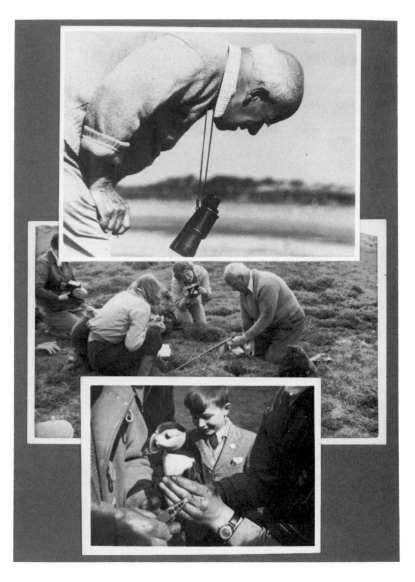

1. The late Eric Ennion wondering whether or not to risk sticking his hand down a Puffin burrow.

2. Having risked it. Note how the expert holds both beak *and* feet . . .

3. . . . and lets somebody else ring it.

Thanks to Hugh Ennion for photos.

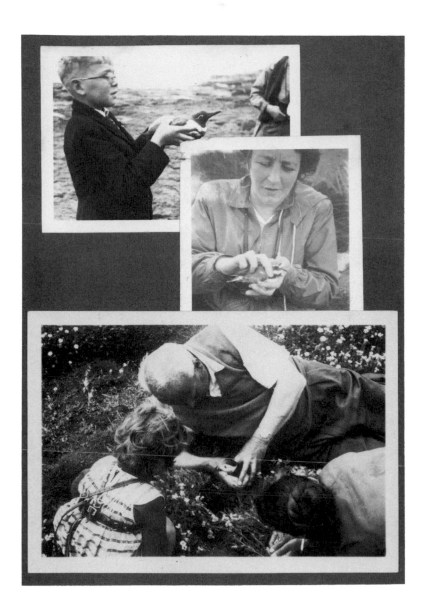

The magic of birds 'in the hand'. 'Bridled' Guillemot and 'Bridled' boy, Ringed Plover, Puffin!

3. ℞ Trapping in Garden.

Species.	Length	(to skull) B.11 (to feathers)	Tail	Tarsus	Wing
SONG THRUSH!	-	18 birds	70 mm?	3.5 mm	116 mm
BLUE TIT.?	-	8 mm	42 mm	18 mm	58 mm
STARLING. ♂♀	-	27 mm	6Q mm	40 mm	130 mm
DUNNOCK	-	12 mm	?	22 mm	68 mm
DUNNOCK	-	Pink on right leg.			
Blackbird.	-	26	99	25?	130

The ringing station at Oak Tree Crescent. **1.** Two superb drop traps cunningly disguised by blackcurrant bushes. **2.** Instant success – a fine House Sparrow. *Photo by Granny.* **3.** Meticulous data.

8
Cley

Back in the fifties Cley-Next-the-Sea, on the north Norfolk coast, was undoubtedly the Mecca of British bird-watching. Fair Isle was almost inaccessible and the Scilly Isles had hardly been discovered. At least once a year, and particularly in the autumn, almost every birder worth the name drove, cycled, hitched or walked to Cley. My experienced mates in the school Natural History Society told me it was so, and the reference books confirmed it. It is entirely appropriate, therefore, that the first wholly written up accounts in my very first big notebook (actually a small green exercise book) record my very first proper bird holiday: 'September 8th to the 15th, 1956, to Cley.'

I was just fifteen. In fact I stayed at Blakeney. I didn't know any better in those days. Blakeney is a small village only a few miles along the coast from Cley. It is more favoured by yachtsmen than bird-watchers and consequently has posher hotels. This no doubt appealed to my father, who came with me on the holiday. Well, I say came with me – he drove me from Birmingham to Blakeney in the first place, and each day he dropped me off at the best bird spots and picked me up in the evenings. I think he spent *his* holiday touring the Norfolk Broads and taking in the scenery. I remember him trying to persuade me that I'd really enjoy a trip to a very pretty village called Potter Heigham, which of course had no appeal to me whatsoever except that it had a silly name. I went with him and sulked. The next day he was only too glad to get rid of me, which is what I wanted. Manipulative little tyke I was.

There are probably not many people reading this book who haven't been to Cley sometime or other. But if you've been there recently let me explain: whatever Cley is like now, it wasn't much like it then. These days the whole area is, in the best sense, highly organised. I suppose the centre of activity is the Norfolk Naturalists Trust Reserve Information Centre just east of the village. This is a great big building housing an exhibition with lovely shiny colourful, photographs illustrating conservation work and the birds that are benefiting. You can buy bird books, car stickers, badges, ties and porcelain Pochards and, of course, permits, which will allow you access to many of the half dozen or so splendidly positioned hides overlooking the adjoining marshes. There is a great big car park and, if that's full, you can nip half a mile down the road to the layby serving the smaller information centre run by the Norfolk Ornithologists Association. They'll tell you what's about, sell you a field-guide to identify it and, if you've forgotten your binoculars, they'll hire you a pair!

Back in 1956 the nearest thing to an information centre was the observatory ringing hut. This was a garden shed perched half way up Whalsey Hill more or less on the site now occupied by the NOA's Headquarters. In the fifties Cley was still an official bird observatory, which it isn't now. There were no dormitories or cooking facilities like Monk's House or Dungeness, but there *was* a hut. Close by, and half hidden by the bushes they were supposed to cover, were two quite large Heligoland traps. Visiting bird-watchers, me included, would pop into the hut to see if anything interesting had been caught that morning. Then we'd set off down the East Bank. The East Bank at Cley is a legend. It is also a bank. It was then, and still is, a long dyke with a path along the top. It is about half a mile long. Due to the reclamation of the marshes, the so-called Coast Road at Cley is rather perversely half a mile away from the sea, so the east bank runs from the road down to the shingle ridge, which hopefully prevents the ocean flooding the flat coastal plain of north Norfolk (as happened in the disastrous East Coast floods of 1952). Either side of the East Bank are marshes. At a glance they don't look much different from the way they were in the fifties but times *have* changed. To the east is Arnold's Marsh: it stretches from the East Bank to what was known as the Iron Road, a parallel track surfaced with strange rusty metal sleepers. Arnold's consists of a couple of large brackish pools and various smaller and muddier patches, some of them fringed by reeds. In the old days access was restricted but not forbidden. It was the best-watched area and produced most of the best birds, especially waders. To the west of the East Bank, opposite Arnold's, was an even more impressive habitat. There was a reed bed and, hidden away shrouded from view, were an untold number of splendid little pools. It was clearly a superb area and it was reasonable to suppose that it attracted many a rare bird. It was known as Billy's Marsh, and we weren't allowed in! This area is now the site of an impressive reserve, owned and managed by the Norfolk Naturalist Trust, and it may well have been then. Anyway, back in 1956 Billy Bishop was the warden. To nervous schoolboys, and maybe to everyone else too, Billy was the Bert Axell of north Norfolk! I'll admit I really never got to know him, I was too frightened. Rumour had it that if you were caught on Billy's Marsh you'd be shot, and it was said that though many a young birder had dared to go in, very few came out. Of course I'm absolutely certain none of this was true. Schoolboys love frightening one another, and themselves. Any fusillade that Billy fired was purely verbal and probably justified. On the other hand, he *did* have a roar like a cannon! Mind you, this was sometimes a blessing. Rare birds, of course, soon got to hear about Billy's Marsh, and would inevitably dive into the safest sanctuary in the East, away from prying binoculars. This wouldn't have bothered us had Billy not had a mildly irritating ability to make sure we *knew* we were permanently dipping out. He rarely actually spoke to us, but the rumours soon spread to the ringing hut.

'Anything about today?'

'Nope.'

'Caught anything?'

'Nope, not a sausage.'

'Nothing on Arnold's?'

'Nope, apparently not. Oh, apparently Billy had a White-rumped this morning.'

'Oh. Where?'

'Guess.'

'Billy's Marsh!'

If we hadn't *known*, it wouldn't have been so bad, but now we *did* know. A White-rumped Sandpiper can hide itself fairly effectively on any one of a dozen mystery pools in the middle of a square mile of reed beds. There wasn't a hope in hell of seeing it from the East Bank or even if we stood on the roof of the ringing hut. What was needed was a volunteer. If Billy wasn't actually visible, it was a fair bet that he was crouching somewhere in the depths of the marsh waiting for trespassers. A brave young birder would step forward and offer to transgress. It really didn't involve much danger. You only had to slide down the East Bank, hop over a ditch and put one wellie on to the bottom rung of the gate. This would provoke a bellowing 'Oi!' that would have drowned out a fieldful of water bailiffs. Bitterns would shoot vertically from the reed beds like jump jets. Bearded Tits would start clanging like alarm bells and, with any luck, the White-rumped would zoom over to the comparative peace of Arnold's Marsh and a hundred appreciative bird-watchers! As always, I'm sure I've been ever so unfair. Nowadays Billy's Marsh is one of the most delightful birding areas in East Anglia. It has been extended and managed, and stands as an obvious credit to years of hard work put in by Mr Bishop Senior. What's more, it is no longer a land of mystery. There are lots of excellent paths and hides, all readily available to the public for the very reasonable price of a permit. The reserve is now run by Billy's son, Bernard Bishop, with an amiable civility that totally lets down the family tradition! White-rumpeds appear nearly every year, and *everyone* sees them.

But let's get back to 1956 and the set-up so far. There was the ringing hut on Whalsey Hill, Arnold's Marsh to the east, Billy's Marsh to the west and down the middle, the legendary East Bank. What was so special about the East Bank? Well, firstly it gave you some good views. You could sit down and scan across the reeds, hoping for a glimpse of one of Billy's rarities, or you could turn round and study visible birds on Arnold's, or you could sprawl out on the far end and have a sea-watch. On my very first day of my first birding holiday, I did all that. My notes at the time reveal a young bird-watcher making some useful observations and some dreadful mistakes:

'The juvenile Ringed Plovers have a chest band that often rarely meets. Care must be taken when Kentish Plover springs to mind; the legs must certainly be noted.'

Fair comment indeed! But then:

'Five Godwits seen in flight, probably Bar-tailed.'

Twit! Were they zooming around on closed wings, then? (N.B. I'm sure you know this but . . . Black-tailed Godwits have whacking great wing bars and black tails; Bar-tails have neither. If you can't identify them in flight . . . well . . . enough said.) And even stranger is a description of a bird flying past off shore which ends up:

'The upper parts (including tail probably) were grey, not very dark nor as light as a Tern, and the underparts whitish. NO BIRD OF THIS SIZE OR DESCRIPTION CAN BE FOUND IN THE FIELD GUIDE!'

My God! A first for Europe! How's that for beginner's luck? Or rather, beginner's inexperience. By the end of the week I'd learnt to recognise autumn plumage Black Terns! What's more, my first day on the East Bank ended with my first major string:

'September 9th: one Grey Phalarope. Grey on back, and orange-brown underparts, whitish face, and black stripe through eye. Underparts: rich orange, not quite meeting the grey.'

Mm really? By the next morning, I'd admitted:

'The Phalarope has gone.'

A day later I was a little more informative:

'East Bank: one Knot!'

But I *still* didn't own up it was the same bird! Real Grey Phalaropes have been seen from the East Bank – though rarely in full breeding plumage! – and so have many other excellent birds. It is indeed a great vantage point, a sort of natural grassy grandstand, with uninterrupted views in all directions. In the fifties you had to get there early to get a good seat. By mid morning there'd be a crowd of maybe forty or more lined up on both sides. It looked like a modern day twitch, yet a crowd on the East Bank in those days didn't mean there was necessarily a rare bird to be seen. It was more a gathering – place for birders to meet, exchange news and talk birds. If something good flew over, then that was a bonus

Black and Bar-tailed Godwits, Knot and Grey Phalarope . . . and Black Terns . . . not necessarily in that order!

and we'd watch it. If not, we'd watch one another. The flock was wonderfully mixed. There'd be lots of young beginners like myself, plus local naturalists, and bird experts not only from Norfolk but from all over the country. I hardly knew them personally but their names were famous: usually double-barrelled or triple initialled – James Ferguson-Lees, Dick Bagnall-Oakley, P.A.D. Hollom and D.I.M. Wallace. Star names from the pages of the *Handbook* and *British Birds*. I couldn't have told you which was which, but I knew they were there. Unlike many birding crowds, there were several women in the ranks. The East Bank provided a splendid horizon along which the silhouettes of local characters could be identified from miles away.

During a subsequent, and rather unsuccessful, September trip in 1961 I amused myself by designing a slim but original volume entitled *Field Guide to the Bird Watchers*. Inside the cover I depicted roadside, or rather East Bank, silhouettes in the manner of the Peterson Field Guides. These featured the outlines of several memorable ladies. There was Mrs Meicklejohn – as tall as a giraffe but with the profile of an eagle – and her companion, whom I think was called Miss James, who was tiny but wore a great big beret and in silhouette resembled a large mushroom. There was the jaunty shape of Elizabeth (Liz) Forster who still lives in the area when she isn't gallivanting up and down the Himalayas in search of adventure and birds (see *The Wandering Tattler* and *Himalayan Solo* both by E. Forster). And there were other people whose names and outlines I've forgotten. Alas, the original *Guide*, which I presented to the observatory at the time (I don't know if they wanted it!), has been long lost. But there was one East Bank silhouette everyone knew. 13 September 1956 my notebook records the vital clue to its identification:

'I saw three men in the stubble field and pursued them and joined them on the bank to wait for Lapland Buntings. One of the men was Mr R.A. Richardson.'

Richard Richardson's silhouette was distinctive enough and, when the light shone on him, so was his dress. It changed so rarely that I presumed he had several indentical sets. It wasn't exactly typical birder's gear, though the fact that he habitually rode a motorbike explained some of it. Richard always wore tight jeans and black leather motorbike boots, a black leather jacket and black beret. Behind him along the bank trotted two tiny hairy little dogs called Midge and Gnat. The trio was quite unmistakable, and their silhouettes could be spotted four miles away through decent binoculars – invaluably convenient for bird-watchers who wished to contact him. Only if the temperature soared to the sub-tropical would Richard remove his leather jacket and reveal a black and white Norwegian-check sweater. It was several years before I discovered to my surprise that he had hair, when I attended a rather stately slide evening in the village hall and, in deference to the occasion, Richard took off his beret. He spoke with a distinctive half stammer that seemed less an impediment than an indication that he was permanently suppressing a tendency to be frivolous. Considering he was such an outstanding and serious ornithological authority, Richard *was* often delightfully frivolous. When he held court on the East Bank, he was less likely to be discussing a tortuous point of identification than cracking a joke or enjoying a gossip about local scandal. It was clear that Richard revelled in the idiosyncrasies of all the various north Norfolk characters, and he was wickedly accurate in impersonating them. The tables were frequently turned. Richard's own voice was so distinctive that it was not hard to impersonate *him*. So most of us did and, indeed, with great affection, still do.

Like Eric Ennion, Richard Richardson was a superb self-taught artist and, also like Dr Ennion, he was endlessly generous in passing on his expertise. He clearly enjoyed teaching, delighting in the naivety and enthusiasm of beginners, and obviously gaining immense satisfaction from helping to improve their skills. He was entirely unacademic. He belonged, more than any other eminent birder I have known, in *the field*. Though he assiduously illustrated every British bird for the Collins *Pocket Guide*, he somehow seemed more in his element sketching on the back of a cigarette packet on the East Bank.

I was privileged to spend many hours over several years birding with Richard. Inevitably I learnt a great deal about birds and about bird-watchers – and how to enliven a boring sea-watch by building up a stack of old tin cans and throwing pebbles at them. But Richard's most invaluable lesson was a strangely negative one: how to risk being wrong. I've stood with Richard and a group of birders at the end of the East Bank and he'd suddenly yell: 'Little Gull! No . . . no, it's only a young Kittiwake.' Thereby admitting that even an expert like him can momentarily make a fundamental error. But though *he* might have made a mistake, the rest of us hadn't seen the bird at all! His eyes were phenomenally quick. He was usually first to spot something interesting, and he immediately shared it and risked a snap identification. The commoner tendency is for birders to let the poorly seen bird disappear and *then* mutter:

'Did anyone else see that? Was it a Little Gull?'

. . . and it's too late then! It's a simple enough lesson, but it requires a rare mixture of confidence and humility: If you see something – *say so*. Have a go and don't worry about being wrong. Of course, at a second glance Richard never *was* wrong. He was simply one of the most impressive field ornithologists Britain has ever produced.

My first meeting with Richard Richardson was on the East Bank in September 1956. My last was twenty years later on Fair Isle in October 1976. At the time we were involved in the tricky business of identifying Britain's first Pallas's Reed Bunting. It gives me great personal satisfaction to recall having been able to show that bird to him. He'd shown *me* an awful lot more! It was also thrilling that he was able to provide the illustration for the official write-up in *British Birds*. Less than a year later he died, at the tragically young age of fifty-five. The greatest of the Norfolk silhouettes was gone, and the East Bank has never been the same.

Meanwhile, back on the morning of 14 September 1956, Mr Richardson told me about the east wind. Norfolk bird-watchers pray for it. Most readers are, I'm sure, familiar with the basic principle. In autumn, migrants are passing from northern Europe, let's say from Norway, down the coasts of Denmark and Holland and onwards, heading south to winter in Africa or even the Middle East. Put simply, if there's an east wind it will blow them across the North Sea, so they end up along the Norfolk coast instead. The whole process is most popularly known as drift migration. There are certain meteorological conditions which are particularly likely to cause this displacement. When the Norfolk birder looks at his *Times* weather map, ideally he hopes to see an anticyclone over Scandinavia. This means nice weather in Norway in which the birds will set off on their southward journey and an east wind to blow them across the North Sea. If there's a bit of rain or fog on the Norfolk coast extending someway offshore, so much the better. The birds will be happily drifting south-east, get caught up and confused in the poor visibility, and look for somewhere to rest. It is now too far to go back to Europe and anyway they'd be flying against that nasty east wind, so they plonk down in Norfolk (and other places on Britain's east coast). If a large number of these migrants *do* arrive, then it is known as a 'fall', and if there's a real avalanche, it's a 'rush'; and hopefully it will include a few rarities. The birds are tired and hungry and they'll descend on the first descent bit of cover they can find. Thus islands, promontories, and isolated coastal patches of trees are most likely to attract a fall, which is why most bird observatories are stuck on islands and promontories. On 14 September 1956 there *was* an anticyclone over Scandinavia. The wind *was* in the east and Mr Richardson told me the promontory to go to was Blakeney Point; there I would surely find good birds, particularly, with any luck, Ortolan Buntings.

It was, and still is, possible to take a boat out to the Point from Morston, but really that was cheating, and anyway the visit would be comparatively short, as the tides restrict the coming and going. The *real* way was to walk. The trek along

Blakeney Point is as much a Norfolk legend as the East Bank. It's a dreadful experience and could appropriately be incorporated into an Outward Bound course. You start at the end of the Cley Beach Road by the Coastguards Station. This used to be the site of the original Cley Bird Observatory, but the premises were washed away in the 1952 floods. You can postpone the awful moment by seawatching for a while by the Coastguards, but eventually the lure of rarities beckons you to turn westward and face the never-ending shingle ridge that stretches away beyond human eyesight. Trekking along the Blakeney Point shingle is like marching through a field of congealed tapioca (something I've had to do in the cause of comedy, so I know). For every foot you put forward, you slide two feet back. It's perfectly possible to walk towards the Point for an hour and end up back at the East Bank. It's even nastier in wellies. Your socks sweat and your arches ache. The first half of the walk is all shingle. No birds . . . just shingle. Then at last you arrive at a derelict building known as Halfway House. You can sit down and shelter there (it's probably drizzling) and it's a comfort, until you realise that 'Halfway House' implies you've still got as far to go as you've already come. At least you can take a break now and look for birds. You probably won't see any immediately but they may well be there. They are lurking in the sueda. Sueda bushes grow thick and quite tall and look like giant flowerless heather, rather like patches of gorse without the prickles. There's a big area of sueda around the Halfway House. They may not have prickles but they are hell to walk through, and they're nearly always soaking wet, either from rain, dew or sea-spray. Understandably, tired migrants hide right in the middle and are impossible to see unless you go in after them. A lot of chivvying and pishing goes on, and even then you are doomed to a series of fleeting tantalising glimpses of little brown birds that are always five yards ahead of you. The general technique was known as 'sueda bashing'. This may sound rather aggressive, but our violence was directed not so much against the birds as the beastly bushes themselves. When you'd emerge from the sueda, having seen nothing and got soaked from head to toe and been scratched to hell, it was some consolation at least to let the bush know what you thought of it by bashing it. There was a particularly productive sueda patch in a small sheltered bay known as the Hood. I looked forward to bashing this bit as it usually produced some birds. It clearly had an illustrious history as two or three tiny Heligoland traps had been built there. They too had been badly damaged by the 1952 floods and were no longer in use by 1956, but their skeletons somehow still represented the likelihood of birds. On 14 September the Hood sueda held several warblers and a few Pied Flycatchers and Redstarts: all evidence that the east wind was doing its job.

The Hood is followed by another bleak and birdless stretch of shingle and then at last you arrive at what might be called the Point itself. You now really start birding in earnest. There's an obvious landmark in the form of a large rusty wreck which is stranded up on a flat area excellent for Wheatears and Pipits. There are several wooden holiday chalets, usually uninhabited by mid September, each with an apologetic little garden of tamarisks and clapped-out flowers that have been battered to death by the salty breezes. Not much cop as gardens, but excellent cover for weary little birds. At the end of the Point is the Valhalla to which every Point-walker gratefully staggers – the café, or, as it's more properly known, the tea-house. You really can enjoy a nice cup of tea and a buttered scone there, or the more typical bird-watchers' diet of a can of Tizer and a Mars bar. After the three-hour walk it's like a blast from an oxygen mask. There's even birds to watch from *inside* the café. Stuffed trophies of glorious pasts on the Point, including a superb

White's Thrush – or was that bought from a taxidermist in Hastings? Anyway, live Black Redstarts and even Red-breasted Flycatchers have been known to hop on to the tea-house doorstep, though they're more likely to be flitting around 'the Lupins'. This is the birder's next stop. The Lupins may not actually *be* lupins, but they *look* like they are. Being autumn, there are no flowers, but there are lots of lupin-like leaves on lupin-like bushes, all entangled in a straggly plot just behind the café. The area is surrounded by a rickety fence, which is superb for migrants to perch on, and traversed by a clothes-line, which is even better. There's a fair scattering of old tin cans and rusty barbed wire – excellent habitat for rare birds – and nowadays there's even a specially provided little drinking pool. On my first visit the lupins were jumping with a nice assortment of Warblers and more Pied Flycatchers and Redstarts but still no Ortolan Buntings; but then we still hadn't looked at 'the Plantation'. Now, the Hood is pretty good, and the lupins are excellent, but the Plantation is what Blakeney Point is really all about.

Remember I mentioned those isolated coastal patches of trees being so attractive, especially if they're on promontories? Well, here we are. The Plantation *is* an isolated patch of trees on a promontory. It's not a big plantation, it's actually about twenty foot square and most of the trees are dead! But it works. This unimpressive mini forest has provided shelter for innumerable rarities over the years. It may be sparse but it's amazing what can hide in it. At first glance it can look birdless but, if you just sit and wait, Warblers and Flycatchers materialise before your very eyes. That's if there's an east wind. On other days it's a complete washout. What materialised before my eyes that September day was neither Flycatcher nor Warbler. It was, yes, perched right on top of the tallest and deadest branch, an Ortolan Bunting.

My notebook records the happy event:
'Through the telescope it could be seen to be a bird of the year'
– and furthermore –
'a male just out of eclipse was seen in Marram'
and
'I saw another immature in the grass. We later saw it again over the other side, and finally obtained excellent views in the trees down to twenty-five feet approximately.'

The notes that follow are, surprisingly perhaps, pretty meticulous:

'Immature: heavy-headed and large – rather ugly – pink red bill – white eye ring, cream moustachial stripes, set off by black underneath. Back strikingly marked, two bars. Little white on tail. Eclipse male: greener darker head, with cream yellow moustache very promiment.'

Even the little drawing is almost recognisable! Well, not bad for a lad who had been stringing Knot for Grey Phalarope a couple of days earlier. I'd come a long way in a week.

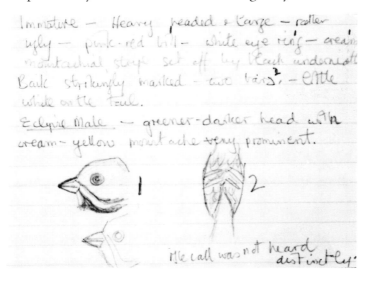

Looking back on my notes from that holiday, and visualising the scene of Blakeney Point, there clearly had been a fall, if not a rush. I have a clear vision of sueda bushes leaping with Willow Warblers and Redstarts flitting from every lupin. I've been back to the Point any number of times over the years and, frankly, I've never again seen anything like it! I enjoyed a fantastic first bird holiday at Cley. I saw 106 species in the week, eighteen of them new to me at the time (and *not* counting that phoney Phalarope). I did see much sub-rarities as Ortolan, Lapland Buntings and Blue Throats, but I've often wondered . . . what did I miss?!!

So . . . what *did* I miss?

From 1957 to 1967 I visited Cley every single year and sometimes two or three visits within the year. I sometimes went on my own, sometimes with school friends and occasionally with my old Bartley companion Andrew Lowe. Even way back then I like to think I had a tendency to 'pioneer' and steer away from the most heavily-watched areas. I started staying not at Cley itself but down the coast a couple of miles, at Salthouse. My theory was that Salthouse marshes looked just as promising as Cley marshes but were being rather neglected, so I booked myself in at the Salthouse Guest House. It was rather musty in those days and it is now closed and almost derelict. Staying at Salthouse and without a car, I avoided the temptation of zipping straight to the East Bank in the mornings and instead religiously plodded around Salthouse marshes each day after breakfast. I never actually saw much really but I did feel ever so self-righteous. Mind you, I also lived in a perpetual state of anxiety. I could see the silhouetted bird watchers a mile away on the East Bank and if one of them so much as raised his binoculars I was convinced I was being gripped off. I probably didn't see much at Salthouse simply because I kept my eyes fixed on the distant horizon! The minute I spotted Richard Richardson's familiar figure I would literally run one and a half miles to catch him before he hopped on his motorbike and went off for tea without telling me what I'd missed. Eventually the strain became too much and I gave in and moved up to Cley with the rest of 'the lads'. There I stayed in a little boarding-house run by a delightful couple, Mr and Mrs Torrington, who fed me enormous meals and allowed me to watch their telly when the wind blew from the west. Once I stayed at The George, the main hotel in Cley, which was in those days almost the unofficial dormitory of the bird observatory.

Over those ten years my visits were spread around the seasons: three in September, one in October, three in November, two in January, three in May and one in June. I always rather felt you were *meant* to go in autumn but, apart from that first holiday, my September visits were the *least* successful. The absolute nadir was in 1961. I decided to celebrate the advent of my longer university holidays by staying at Cley right through to the day before I was due back at Cambridge. I was there from 8 September to 2 October – over three flipping weeks! I limped to the Point and back nearly every day and saw nothing. The east wind blew for only two days out of twenty-four, and then it was off a local depression and no Scandinavian migrant even thought about crossing the North Sea. I was reduced to forsaking the area and hitching lifts to East Anglian twitches. I went to Wisbech Sewage Farm and dipped out on a Pectoral Sandpiper. My only 'luck' was to be the five hundredth person to see a Baird's Sandpiper at the unlikely venue of a gravel pit by the A1 at Wyboston. At the time, this was a very rare bird – the fourth British record, I think. Have Bairds become commoner, or is it merely an indication of increased observer coverage that nowadays four in a year would not be remarkable? In recent times, I've even found two myself and have seen maybe a dozen, including three together in southern Ireland. It's funny how some rarities seem to avoid you all your life (I've only just seen *my* first White-rumped) whilst others almost follow you. But *nothing* followed me in September 1961 except gloom and depression. I tried hard to fight it off. I tried to string a 'funny Starling' into a Rosy (Roseate Starling, that is – a rare one). I spent more time on my notebooks and they became increasingly ornate. I decorated them hopefully with newspaper cuttings of the European weather-maps. I slaved over my *Field Guide to the Bird Watchers*, and I even consumed a day or two composing a Bird Anthem: 'Seventy-six Greenshanks', to the tune of *Seventy-six Trombones* (See *Bill Oddie's Little Black Bird Book*, 'The Birders' Song Book', page 143). All to no avail. It just got worse and worse, including the

weather. As always my notebook finally summed it up:
'30th September: all wet 'n 'orrible. Telly.'

At other times of the year I was much more successful. In 1964 I took my first spring birding holiday, from 23 May to the 29th. It was very good indeed, and I find it inexplicable that it took me another ten years to realise that I actually prefer birding holidays in spring rather than the autumn. The birds are in superb plumage, there's often more of them and yet there are fewer birdwatchers. Nowadays every spring I go down to Scilly or up to Shetland. They rarely fail me. Those are stories yet to be told. In May 1964 in Norfolk I had a feast of good birds: Mediterranean Gull, a superb male Montagu's Harrier, Quail, a Red-breasted Flycatcher that actually had a red breast, and a magnificent male Woodchat Shrike. Yet the bird I remember best of all was strictly speaking not an acceptable pukka rarity at all. 25 May, a lovely sunny morning, wind east force three to four: and flitting around in the field by the East Bank, amongst a flock of newly arrived Yellow Wagtails, a dazzling male of the Scandinavian Grey-headed Race. My own delight and excitement was echoed by Richard Richardson who had not seen such a bird at Cley for over ten years. And yet . . .

My *very best* trips to Cley were during the winter.

The north Norfolk coast is flat and bleak and can be dreadfully desolate. Bird-watching can be hard and chilly work, but it's often magnificently rewarding and extremely memorable. Not only do I recall the specific good birds I saw, but also some really vivid visual images, created from a combination of the scenery, the weather and the wild life. Within a few months of my first September trip I was back at Salthouse Guesthouse for ten days in January 1957, enjoying swirls of Snow Buntings living up to their name as they cascaded from cold, grey winter skies. How thoughtful (if corny) of the Creator to give Snow Buntings flight-calls like jingle bells! My meanderings around Salthouse marshes were rewarded with great views of Shore Larks creeping around the shingle, black and yellow males looking like a strange hybrid between a mouse and an overgrown wasp. Brent Geese in a snowstorm – instant Peter Scott – and four thousand Wigeon rising from Billy's Marsh like a plague of startled locusts. I had one frustration. In January 1957 I began a quest that was to haunt me for nearly ten years: to see a Great Grey Shrike on Salthouse Heath. People were always seeing them: 'Great Grey on the Heath this morning,' but by the time I'd got there it was always a tale of 'Oh, you should have been here an hour ago, it was perched on the signpost at the cross roads.' Year after year I wandered Salthouse Heath thinking, 'Where would I be now if I were a Shrike?' I sat by every signpost and I scanned every sprig of charred gorse, but I never saw a Great Grey Shrike. Until October 1966, when fate gave up with a huge sigh and, as if feeling guilty for past cruelties, awarded me four Great Grey Shrikes in the space of two days! Mind you, none of them were actually on the Heath: there were two on the Point and two at Holkham.

In January 1958 I was back again for another ten days and, looking back on it, it was perhaps the best period I've ever spent at Cley; though, curiously, I didn't entirely realise *how* good it was till many years later. There was a veritable epidemic of wintering Buntings: a huge mixed flock of nearly two thousand birds foraged in the stubble-field behind Whalsey Hill, including lots of Bramblings, a few Laplands and a splendid avalanche of four hundred Snow Buntings. I also had three wonderfully contrasting 'firsts'. I quote my notes:

'January 8th. Overstrand. (Weather: sunny but immaterial.) Habitat: a walled garden on the edge of a sea cliff by a minor road – the grounds of a "home". Lawns and bushes, ornamental pools etc. Tall trees abundant, with many tall conifers. Two *Collared Doves*!'

Nowadays such a sighting would probably provoke a

scream of indifference. There are now Collared Doves all over Britain, in every farmyard, park and garden, from London to Ireland. But in 1958, only twenty-five years ago, this pair at Overstrand were two of the very first. There's a lovely painting by Richard Richardson commemorating the event on the cover of *British Birds* for June 1957. 'Collared Doves in Norfolk – a bird new to British List.' Collared Doves were hardly a startling-looking bird even then. Nowadays bird-watchers look straight through them, though it's hard to ignore them when they make those nasty noises during the breeding season. Still, they do represent a remarkable success story, but I hope they don't overdo it. Look what happened to the Passenger Pigeon! I can't say I actually recall the look of my first Collared Doves very vividly, but my second 'new bird' of the trip I shall never forget.

9 January, the morning after my first real rarity, I hitched a lift from Salthouse up to the East Bank. A bit idle of me, but it was rather cold. The car suddenly screeched to a halt. There in the field by Billy's Marsh, not a hundred yards away from us, was a haystack, where the previous night there had been merely grass. The car window lowered and four pairs of trembling binoculars peered out. The 'haystack' shuffled on its unfeathered yellow legs, and its steely eyes peered back at us over the biggest hooked beak you ever did see. My notebook records my thought at the time:

'It was obviously an Eagle.'

How's that for instant identification? It was indeed an immature White-tailed Eagle, and, to quote the twitcher's apt phraseology, a crippler if ever there was one! It turned out that some lucky birder had reported a brief sighting of a Sea Eagle a few days before but, since it hadn't been seen again, I guess we'd all been trying to convince ourselves it had been string on a grand scale. Thank God it wasn't. There it was, sitting in a field, so close it was almost frightening. We visibly cowered as it lumbered off the ground and flapped towards Salthouse. My notes continue:

'It appeared at least twice as large as a Shelduck.' What an understatement! As I remember it, it actually looked twice as large as a *house*! Three days later, when it flew over barely fifty feet above our heads, it looked as big as a jumbo jet! Funny to think that, at the time, it was less rare than a Collared Dove . . .

White-tailed Sea Haystack with Collared Doves and . . . something else.

Later that day I saw something even rarer, though I didn't know it at the time and nobody else was quite sure either. When I first saw the bird I came to a conclusion that I could not have been blamed for:

'Returning to the East Bank, I spotted a Harrier – an immature or female Ringtail – flying low over the reeds. After some agile sprinting behind the cover of a dyke, I saw the bird at some twenty yards range. In general plumage it was obviously a Hen or Montagu's. However, I have seen Montagus before and this appeared rather larger and stockier, with wider rather than longer wings. Furthermore, the white on the rump was very vivid and extensive. These points lead me to identify the bird as a Female Hen Harrier.'

Opposite this apparently reasonable conclusion is a subsequent note:

'The Harrier opposite has been in the area some time. It has been observed to have rich apricot-coloured underparts (which I also noted) and, so I am told, these are unstreaked. Many experts, R.A. Richardson, Ferguson-Lees etc., have seen the bird and think that it maybe an immature Pallid Harrier.'

Under that is an additional comment:

'Experts who have seen Pallid think this bird is too stout for that species.'

And underneath *that* I have written, in different coloured ink, and obviously some time later:

'R.A. Richardson says the bird was never absolutely certainly identified, but was probably an American Marsh Hawk.'

The fact was that this bird was the subject of one of the most convoluted identification wrangles known to British ornithology. It was watched, drawn, painted and photographed, and attempts were made to catch it before it finally left Cley after spending the whole winter there outfoxing everyone. It was then discussed on and off for thirteen years,

until all the evidence was corrolated and set against sub-
sequent experience by master bird-sleuth D.I.M. Wallace. In
British Birds, December 1971, the verdict was announced:
'American Marsh Hawk in Norfolk.' Another bird new to
Britain! Thus it was that I finally realised just *how* good that
1958 holiday had been!

By permission of D.I.M. Wallace and British
Birds – *the essential monthly magazine (for free
sample write to Erika Sharrock, Fountains, Park
Lane, Blunham, Bedford MK44 3NJ).*

During my time at university I acquired the habit of escaping the relatively short distance from Cambridge to north Norfolk for occasional weekend trips. Three of these visits were in mid-November and they were all excellent. In 1962 I enjoyed pretending to be a rabbit and being hovered over by a Rough-legged Buzzard, who was either very hungry or had a splendid sense of humour. There was also a typically tame Grey Phalarope (not a Knot) on the little pool by the Coast Guards. In 1965 Cley village was like a Christmas card, with snow frosting the hawthorn bushes whose berries were being gobbled up by Waxwings. There was also a Grey Phalarope at Coast Guards. In 1967, again mid-November, I was back at Coast Guards yet again, and the Grey Phalarope was *still* there. I apologised for failing to visit it the previous year, and drove off to scrutinise the wild-fowl on Billy's Marsh. I wasn't really much in the habit of looking at Ducks very thoroughly. I tended to assume that they were all Wigeon and Teal, with a few Pintail, Gadwall and Shoveler thrown in for luck. But that day some instinct must have suggested I look harder. I was with Andrew Lowe. He and I propped our telescopes on top of the car roof and began systematically scanning through the three hundred Wigeon grazing on the water meadow. I find there is only one way to check a large flock thoroughly and that is to mutter the identification of every single bird: 'Wigeon, Wigeon, Wigeon, Teal, Wigeon, Wigeon, Wigeon, another Wigeon, more Wigeon and . . . what the ★★★!' I don't recall which of us swore first, but it was certainly not in anger. There, amongst the familiar chestnut heads of the European Wigeon, was a green one – no, not a Mallard – a spruce, full plumaged, male American Wigeon. Anxious to share our joy, we were rather pleased when another bird watcher drove past. We waved him to stop and pointed his binoculars in the right direction for him.

'American Wigeon out there. One hundred yards away, to the left of the gatepost.'

'I can't see it.'

'Go to the right hand end of flock, and come back this way.'

'Where?'

'By the Pintail.'

'What Pintail?'

'The male in the middle. Next to that. American Wigeon.'

'Are you sure?'

'Oh course I'm sure. Look, see that clump of reeds?'

'I can see ordinary Wigeon.'

'So can we. There's three hundred of them! And right in the middle there's an American Wigeon. By the clump of reeds.'

'Is it a male?'

'Yes. A male. A male American Wigeon.'

'Hmm. There's a Teal out there.'

'There's five hundred Teal; but there's only one American Wigeon. There, in the middle, with its head up; green head, cream stripe on the forehead. Can't you see it?'

'No.'

'Oh ★★★!'

He drove off. I'm honestly not sure if he *ever* saw it, or perhaps he wouldn't have known what it was if he had done. Fortunately, as *he* drove off, Richard Richardson skidded up to us on his motor bike. He had realised we'd 'got something' by the way we'd gone all red and excited:

'Richard – American Wigeon!'

'Wh-wh-where?'

'There.'

'Got it. Oh yes. Boo-boo-bootiful!'

A few minutes later the flock was disturbed (maybe Billy Bishop was chasing them off his marsh). The Ducks flew off and in the middle of them our bird – free-flying, no sign of wing clipping – surely a genuine wild vagrant. A first for Norfolk, a first for Richard and of course a first for me. It was a very significant first, too. The first proper genuine British rarity I'd actually found myself.

American Wigeon *Anas americana*

> **Norfolk:** Cley, ♂, 15th November (A.R. Lowe, W.E. Oddie, R.A. Richardson et al.).

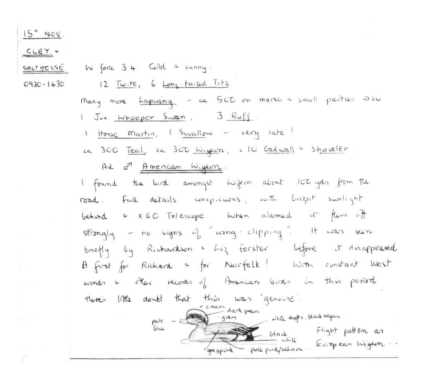

15ᵗ NOV.

CLEY +

SALTHOUSE

0930-1430

W force 3 4. Cold & sunny.

12 Twite, 6 Long-tailed Tits

Many more Lapwing – ca 500 on marsh & small pastures →W

1 Juv. Whooper Swan, 3 Ruff.

1 House Martin, 1 Swallow – very late!

ca 300 Teal, ca 300 Wigeon, c 10 Gadwall & Shoveler.

Ad ♂ American Wigeon.

I found the bird amongst Wigeon about 100 yds from the road. Full details conspicuous, with bright sunlight behind & x 60 Telescope. When alarmed it flew off strongly – no signs of "wing-clipping". It was seen briefly by Richardson & Liz Forster before it disappeared. A first for Richard & for Norfolk! With constant West winds & other records of American birds in this period there's little doubt that this was 'genuine'.

In a way it sort of marked the end of an era in my birding life, and perhaps the beginning of a new one. Maybe I felt it was the culmination of a period of 'qualification'. It was as if I'd finished my training and, at the ripe old age of twenty-six,

I'd finally become a real birder. I'd learnt how to dip out, get gripped off and even how to string. I'd also got my name in *BB*. My fascination with migration and rarities was totally confirmed. I didn't return to Cley for ten years and when I did Richard Richardson was no longer alive. Appropriately, Andrew Lowe was mine host at The George, making a valiant effort to restore it to its rightful state as the unofficial bird observatory. There was log book, not only full of 'recent reports', but defaced with wonderfully scathing comments by sceptical birders. Nearly every good bird was labelled 'stringy' by those who hadn't seen it. There were lots of young bird-boys at the bar: more than in my day and definitely far more expert. All of them seemed to bear nicknames or titles, some seemingly complimentary – such as 'Captain Ticker' – and some not – 'The Incredible String Band!' The whole language of birding had clearly changed; and for a full explanation of that I can only immodestly suggest you read my first book, *Bill Oddie's Little Black Bird Book*.

I was at The George in 1977, and in fact I then got the feeling that Cley was still very much a Mecca of British bird watching, even if it was becoming rapidly eclipsed by the Scilly Isles. At least there were still lots of bird-watchers from all over the country choosing to spend their autumn holidays in north Norfolk. Unfortunately they didn't spend much of their money, and Andrew's efforts to run a profitable hotel for a clientele who tended to buy a pint of Brown Ale and a dozen straws was sadly doomed to failure.

Five years later I was in Cley again. It was like a ghost town. 1 October 1982, right at the peak of autumn migration. Admittedly the wind was from the west and there weren't a lot of birds around, but where were the bird-watchers? Certainly the reserve car park was full and the information centre was doing a roaring trade in ties and permits. There were lots of folk in the hides, but most of

them were snug in their fleece-lined Barbour jackets, trying
to figure out what they were looking at from the pictures in
the latest *Reader's Digest Bird Guide*. Very nice people they
were too, enjoying their birds, and perhaps more so quite
simply because they didn't realise there actually 'wasn't much
about'. But be honest – and I don't mean it at all insultingly –
they were a bunch of dudes! So where were the 'heavy'
birders? Down the East Bank? I drove there and walked it –
alone. Were they in the bar of The George perhaps? No way.
That's now pretty dude too – and very nice it is, mind you!
Try Nancy's Caff, then. Nancy's – a cosy and very friendly
little tea-room – provides the unofficial (or possibly official)
information service to the nation's twitchers – the young
(and not so young) new wave of bird-watchers who will
travel night and day as far as is necessary whenever or
wherever there's a rare bird to be seen. If there are good birds
in the Cley area, then Nancy's will be packed with
celebrating revellers. If not, it'll be almost empty. On 1
October 1982 there were *two* birders in there. Two guys who
lived locally and, as they put it, 'couldn't afford to go
twitching that week'. The phone rang frequently, calls from
London, Teeside, Bristol: 'Anything about?' This didn't
necessarily mean 'Anything in Norfolk?' It meant 'Anything, anywhere?' All the information was jotted down in a
book at Nancy's:

'Er . . . Sharp-tailed in Cheshire . . . probably gone . . .
Purple Heron at Mins . . . White-rumped in Cornwall . . .
No news from Fair Isle . . . it's all in the Scillies really . . .
Red-eyed Vireo, possibly Olivaceous, and definite Water
Thrush.'

'OK. Thanks. I'll try and get down for the weekend.'

'Here?'

'No. Scillies.'

As he put the phone down the informant explained: 'Very
few people actually *stay* in Cley now. They just pass through

on their way to somewhere else. It's not like the old days.'

It may not be, but maybe that's not *such* a bad thing. The Norfolk coast is still one of the very finest bird-watching areas in Britain. In fact, I think it's even better than it was in the fifties. There are superb reserves at Snettisham, Holme, Titchwell and Cley – valuable habitats that have not only been conserved but improved. The birds appreciate it and so do the hundreds of less frantic bird-watchers who visit the area every year. To any young birder, wishing to gain fundamental experience of a wide variety of species, who asks me where is the best place to go, my answer would definitely be . . . Cley.

1. Mystery photo – easy . . .Full plumaged adult R.A. Richardson.   **2.** An East Bank Team Photo 1951, a younger Richard third from left.   **3.** With young Marsh Harrier.   **4.** Outside the original Cley Bird Observatory's ringing hut, 1955.   **5.** Richard on a hot day.   **6.** Racing home for tea.
Thanks for photos to Peter Clarke and Paul Kirkby.

Cley-Next-the-Sea

Where I stayed: 1. Salthouse guest house. **2.** Mrs Torrington's. **3.** The George. **4.** The East Bank – 9 October 1982 – no birders. **5.** Arnold's Marsh – also 1 October – no birds.

6. Great Grey Shrike (race gigantieus plywoodus) always a 'cert' at the Norfolk Ornithologists Association reserve at Holme (very good for real birds too). **7.** Salthouse Heath . . . Shrike-less signpost.

The journey to the Point   **1.** The pool by the Coastguards. I didn't bother to identify the little dot by the left-hand shore – it was presumably a Grey Phalarope.   **2.** Delaying the dreadful moment by sea-watching. 'The Point' is out there to the west.   **3.** Low-angle view of shingle taken by crawling birder – me.   **4.** Close-up of sueda bush as seen by an exhausted bird – or bird-watcher (again, me).   **5.** Halfway House.

The journey to the Point   6. The second half. . . .   7. The Tea House; and 'the lupins', in which there was, on this particular day, one Wren!   8. The Plantation . . . being scrutinised by another bird-watcher. Which made two of us. One more than the number of birds.   9. The other side of the plantation – looking back on the two-hour return journey.

Cley today

1. NNT Visitor Centre – this picture had to be taken just before 7.00 am on a wet Monday in early December – the only time the building is not entirely obliterated by 'dudes'.

2. Nancy's Café . . . on a day when . . .

3. Everything was on the Scillies!

The last bit

When I started work on this book I had a plan. I was determined to write about *birds*, and I hope I've done that. I also intended to cover *all* my various holidays, travels and expeditions; but here I am at page 180 already. As one who has rarely been capable of reading anything longer than *British Birds*, and finds the *Beano* a bit heavy-going, I feel I have a moral obligation to keep my own book fairly short. Also, as my publisher reminds me, I must keep it portable. I'm not sure why. I don't want anyone pulling any muscles carrying it out of the shop, I suppose. More to the point, the *longer* a book becomes, the *more* they'll charge you for it! And, ever mindful that bird-watchers' money is better spent on petrol, plane tickets and new binoculars, I don't want to push my luck. If you've got this far, I hope you've actually bought this book yourself and, if you *have*, thank you. I hope you've enjoyed reading it as much as, I admit, I've enjoyed writing it. If you *have* enjoyed it, then I assume you'll be pleased to hear that I'm already thinking about the next one. If you *haven't* enjoyed it then . . . you won't even have got this far. So I won't bother telling you that the next one will cover the Scillies and Fair Isle and Ireland and . . . anywhere that I could only get to by *crossing a stretch of water*. I have just decided that this is my ridiculously spurious criterion for deciding to finish *this* book where I have and for now writing . . .

THE END
and good birding
BILL ODDIE